seedheads

in the garden

seedheads

in the garden

Noël Kingsbury

photographs by Jo Whitworth

TIMBER
PRESS

In memory of Lesley Rosser (1955–2006), whose gardens brought joy to many
and whose teaching, at the English Gardening School and elsewhere,
brought horticultural knowledge and inspiration to budding designers.

Published in 2006 by Timber Press

Timber Press, Inc.

The Haseltine Building

133 S.W. Second Avenue, Suite 450

Portland, Oregon 97204-3527, U.S.A.

www.timberpress.com

For contact information regarding editorial, marketing, sales,

and distribution in the United Kingdom, see www.timberpress.co.uk

ISBN-13 978-0-88192-796-2

ISBN-10 0-88192-796-1

Designed by Ruth Hope

Printed through Colorcraft Ltd., Hong Kong

Library of Congress Cataloging-in-Publication Data

Kingsbury, Noël.

Seedheads in the garden / Noël Kingsbury; photographs by Jo Whitworth.

p. cm.

Includes bibliographical references and index.

ISBN-13: 978-0-88192-796-2

ISBN-10: 0-88192-796-1

1. Seedheads. 2. Seedheads--Ecology. 3. Native plants for

cultivation--Seeds. I. Title.

SB439.28.K56 2006

635.9--dc22

2006005925

A catalog record for this book is also available from the British Library.

Contents

Foreword

Noël Kingsbury continues to enrich our garden libraries with references that are as useful as they are beautiful. This time he has devoted an entire book to a long-neglected matter that is close to my heart – the beauty of the garden in autumn.

It is early August as I write, and I am looking over my own summer garden, which is located on the eastern shore of the Chesapeake Bay near St. Michaels, Maryland, in the United States. Hints of autumn already pervade the scene. The elongated black discs of *Rudbeckia maxima* seedheads, which stand head high, bob up and down under the weight of grasshopper sparrows and finches that have come to feast. Other beautiful colors are starting to emerge as well. The long seedpods of *Thermopsis villosa* are chocolate-brown, and the dried *Hydrangea quercifolia* blossoms are mauve. It is difficult to resist picking these autumn riches before their time.

I am enchanted by an entire book devoted to the beauty of the autumn garden, especially one that emphasizes the seadheads themselves. This book boldly illustrates that autumn is equally as important in garden beauty and interest as spring or summer. Instead of the traditional evergreen, which is often thought of as 'alive', the natural fall garden offers a plethora of colors, from crimson and gold to charcoals and black. And, of course, the exuberance of autumn foretells winter – the year's final garden display that I like to describe as a 'dried bouquet'.

As the title implies, however, this book offers much more than an understanding of the autumn garden. I learned a great deal from the author's description of 'the botany of seedheads' and his section on cultivation. The detailed knowledge gained from these discussions already has enriched my understanding and appreciation of autumn gardening, especially as it relates to my practice. Who will not be intrigued to study the botany of their own garden more closely?

In the Plant Directory that follows these informative opening chapters, the author provides a complete reference for creating gardens that are glorious in all seasons, but especially so in autumn and even into winter.

Until now fall gardens have been predominantly evergreen. I call it the funereal evergreen look. I congratulate Noël Kingsbury for offering a fresh alternative.

James van Sweden
Sherwood, Maryland, USA

Introducing Seedheads

'A plant,' says Dutch garden designer Piet Oudolf, 'is only worth growing if it looks good when it is dead.' His comment is made only half in jest, as he is among a number of innovators who are trying to draw the attention of gardeners and landscape designers to what plants look like long after they have passed their 'best'. Thinking about the winter aspect of plants, and considering their design potential at this time of year, is part of a fundamental change in attitude towards ornamental plants which has been gathering in strength during the 'millennium years'. Seedheads are the key part of a plant's appearance during autumn and winter, and it is to seedheads that this book is devoted.

A good way to start thinking about seedheads is to look at them in nature. Take a winter walk in an environment where you can find a wide variety of wildflowers: paths along the edges of woodland, grassland such as meadow or prairie, or even waste ground in areas of urban or industrial dereliction. See how many attractive or interesting-looking seedheads you can find. How many of them are worth picking to use in dried flower arrangements back at home? How many might be even be worth including in the garden, if you could be sure that they would take to cultivation? Take time to look for interesting shapes and forms, and notice how seedheads often make an impact because you see lots of them at once, and how they look in different kinds of light. Notice in particular how some are very dark, others very light; how some have hard, definite shapes and others are wispy and nebulous, and how these different characteristics can combine to form very attractive compositions.

Often, looking at seedheads in nature involves looking at them growing *en masse*.

But cutting them and including them in a winter floral arrangement is an opportunity to examine them at close hand. This can be very rewarding, as a whole wealth of detail is revealed. Many have shapes of great intricacy, the existence of which would never be guessed at without taking some special effort. The photography in this book illustrates both these aspects of seedheads.

Our aim is to encourage gardeners, garden designers and landscape architects to consider how they can use plants with interesting seedheads in their work. The emphasis is very much on herbaceous perennials, for it is these that form the largest group of plants with good seedheads among the ornamental hardy flora. Seedheads – like flowers – form a substantial part of their visual impact, whereas they are little more than extra ornamentation on those woody plants which have them. The seedheads of herbaceous plants can also make a substantial contribution to the overall visual impact of a garden or other planted space

left The muscular umbels of *Achillea filipendulina* 'Gold Plate' silhouetted against the light heads of a *Calamagrostis* grass.

opposite *Miscanthus sinensis* 'Juli' is one of many varieties of this most decorative and reliable ornamental grass that can look its best in winter.

from mid-autumn to the end of winter – and as such should be regarded as a major source of material for the planting designer.

A discussion of the design aspects of seedheads is the primary mission of this book, but we start off with a look at what exactly they are, their botanical details and the role they play in how plants reproduce themselves – their place in the ecology of plants, in other words. We also look at how seedheads in the garden contribute to the wider ecology: how they can be a food resource for wildlife, and in particular how they can be part of a strategy for attracting birds into the garden.

First, though, we will look briefly at seedheads in garden history. To be more accurate, we will consider their place in what has been a fundamental change in the way that people garden and in how they manage planted landscapes.

For most of garden history, the role of plants in gardens has been heavily controlled. Traditional garden style in every culture which has raised gardening to an art form (European/Christian, Islamic, Chinese, Japanese, south-east Asian) has primarily used plants as a basis for structure or sculpture in the form of clipped hedges, stylized shapes (as in east Asian cloud pruning) or topiary, and has secondarily included flowers and foliage for their decorative properties. Seedheads have rarely featured in traditional garden art. Once a flower has died, it is regarded as being 'over' and is often removed, preventing a

Eryngium giganteum and a *Monarda* variety in frosty weather — the contribution seedheads can make to the winter garden is enormous.

seedhead from forming. The large labour force available to the wealthy elites who were the only people who could afford to make gardens in traditional societies helped to ensure that seedheads rarely made an appearance in the garden.

During the late nineteenth century, however, attitudes began to change. A number of grasses appeared in cultivation, although few of them were widely grown. The key thing about grasses, of course, is that their seedheads are as important a feature of their decorative aspect as their flowers, and in many cases more so. Towards the end of the nineteenth century and in the early years of the twentieth, a number of writers on gardening matters began to promote a much 'wilder' style of growing ornamental plants than the highly organized, indeed almost regimented, style which had been the norm. William Robinson in Britain and Ernst Graf Silva Tarouca in Austria-Hungary both advanced the idea of mixing ornamental perennials with native vegetation and of combining plants in ways which were inspired by natural plant communities.

The role of flower-arrangers in the history of garden design has been much underestimated. As an example of this, it is worth considering that it was flower-arrangers who first began to realize the value of seedheads in making arrangements for the winter months. The small-scale commercial growing of plants such as

Monardas are useful plants, not only flowering in August when there is little else in the perennial border, but also for their strong stems that support distinctive seedheads for most of the winter.

poppies, love-in-a-mist (*Nigella* species), honesty (*Lunaria annua*) and grasses for drying and sale to flower-arrangers began during the 1960s, and possibly even earlier. Increasingly, gardeners began to see their value as garden elements, too.

A widespread appreciation of the value of seedheads had to wait for a change in the way herbaceous perennials were used and, indeed, in the kind of herbaceous plants which were grown in gardens. Herbaceous perennials began to become popular during the latter part of the nineteenth century and arguably reached a peak in their use during the early twentieth century in Britain and in Germany. Many of these were, however, plants which needed a high level of maintenance, and during the years after the Second World War, the rising cost of labour reduced their popularity. During the 1960s and 1970s a wider range of herbaceous perennials and grasses began to be used in Germany, and from the 1970s in Britain, too. The older high-maintenance perennials, typified by Michaelmas daisies (*Aster novi-belgii*), began to be displaced by more robust, longer-lived plants. Many of these were either wild species or cultivars of wild species which retained the natural grace and elegance of their wild ancestors. In some cases these are more likely to produce seedheads containing viable seed, as some hybrids – those with double flowers, especially – are not fertile.

From the 1970s onwards some very innovative designers began to develop a new and distinctly more naturalistic planting style. The key inspirational figure here had in fact been the German nurseryman and writer Karl Foerster (1874–1970), who from the 1930s on had been promoting a wilder look and drawing the attention of gardeners to the subtle charms of ferns and grasses. Foerster was an inspiration for Wolfgang Oehme, who with James van Sweden, from 1975 on, developed a style of planting characterized as being 'bold, romantic and American' and which had a role for seedheads as a major decorative element during the long cold winters typical of the East Coast of the United States. Foerster was also an important inspiration for Piet Oudolf in the Netherlands, who has developed a highly distinctive use of perennials and grasses and has gone on to undertake commissions, mostly for public spaces, in Sweden, Britain and the USA. Oudolf is a first-class photographer of his work, and his photographs of seedheads, often edged in frost, have brought the value of the winter aspect of herbaceous plants to a much wider public, and stimulated a whole new genre of plant and garden photography.

One of Foerster's pupils, Richard Hansen, went on to become director of the Weihenstephan Institute in Bavaria, Germany, where he developed a very rigorously researched planting style based on matching plant species with appropriate garden habitats. Seedheads and winter appearance played an important role in many of these very naturalistic planting combinations, which have achieved a high public profile through their use in garden shows and public parks.

The combined impact of the German perennial planting style, the work of Piet Oudolf and that of Oehme–van Sweden Associates on the gardening public and those more plant-aware members of the landscape profession has been profound. The use of herbaceous perennials in a softer more naturalistic style has become much more widespread and is developing rapidly. There is a feeling, though, that it is still very much in its infancy.

Behind the new wave of perennial-centred planting stands a major political and cultural development – that of the ecology movement. An awareness of the damage done to the natural world by the human race has led to a widespread desire to create more space for nature in urban areas. Nature itself has been accorded a higher value and respected more, as part of which attitudes to garden plants have changed. 'We no longer regard every yellow leaf as a sign of disease or failure,' says Dutch garden designer and writer Henk Gerritsen, who has been one of the most daring in letting plants run to seed in his garden. The point that he and others – mostly gardeners in the Netherlands and Germany – began to make in the 1970s and 1980s was that gardens do not have to consist always of perfect and colourful flowers or neat shrubs. Plants can look attractive when they are 'over', too, and this, of course, leads us straight to seedheads. There is a definite steak of iconoclasm in the approach of Gerritsen and others who have stressed the importance of seedheads. Traditional practice promoted the removal of spent flowerheads by deadheading partly to promote more flowering, but also for reasons of tidiness.

opposite *Iris* species nearly always have distinctive seedheads which withstand wet and windy weather well.

Botany and Ecology

The 'selfish gene' has become a key concept in the way we look at plant and animal species. Essentially it presupposes that the primary goal of each individual plant and animal is not its own survival but that of the species as a whole, through the medium of its genetic material. Whatever the individual does is thus aimed at preserving – and distributing as effectively as possible – its genes.

Among the flowering plants, it is the seed which is the primary distributor of genes. Seeds are designed to be spread at some distance from the parent plant so as to minimize parent/seedling competition and to be stable, self-contained entities until such time as they meet with conditions which are favourable to germination. At that point they break open and start to grow; from then on they are dependent upon their environment.

above *Monarda* 'Neon' with a beetle. Seedheads provide shelter and food for a wide variety of insects. For the farmer or the seed collector, insect predation of seeds is a problem, but there are no such worries for the ornamental gardener, who can simply enjoy the resulting biodiversity.

Seedheads are those structures which develop after the fertilization of a flower. In the case of nearly all flowering perennials, this is carried out by insects, whereas in the case of grasses and other grass-like plants it is effected by the wind. A seedhead has two main functions: to protect the seed while it develops and then, once it has matured, to distribute it. How effectively this distribution happens is very largely a function of the design of the seedhead: the better the seedhead is at spreading its load of seed far and wide, the more effective it is at distributing the plant's genes. Most seeds are passive and when released from the seedhead simply fall. Once they have landed they rarely move very far. Some, however, play a more active role in their distribution. They may have hooks which cling on to animal fur and enable them to be carried a considerable distance, or they may have appendages which catch the wind and so transport the seed far from the parent plant. Achieving wider distribution accomplishes two things: the reduction in the likelihood that the seedlings will be overshadowed by the parent plant, and the

dissemination of the plant's genes across a geographically larger area, offering a range of possible opportunities to grow and to spread the species.

Here we will consider the basic morphology of seedheads, and to some extent of seeds, very much from the viewpoint of the gardener and designer. In other words, we will look at morphology through aesthetics.

The botany of seedheads

After fertilization, the ovules contained in the ovary grow to become seeds, while the ovary itself (and sometimes other parts of the floral structure) develops into a fruit. In some cases the fruit and the coat of the seed fuse, so that it appears as if the seeds are borne exposed to the world, whereas what we see is in fact a combined seed and seedhead. These are called *achenes*. In some cases, the achene develops structures which enable it to be carried off on the wind: for example, the *pappus*, a minute,

opposite *Aster macrophyllus* 'Twilight' is typical of those daisy-family species with seeds designed to be blown away.

hairy structure in the flower, develops into a feathery structure which acts as a parachute. This is particularly characteristic of the daisy family, the Asteraceae, formerly known as the Compositae. In this family, the achenes are positioned on a structure called the *involucre*, which in fact started off life as the base of a compact compound flowerhead, for daisy-family 'flowers' are composed of many separate tiny individual flowers, each one called a *floret*. In the case of *Clematis* and *Pulsatilla* (both members of the Ranunculaceae), the long hairy structure which catches the wind is derived from the old *style* of the flower – the structure which transported the fertilizing pollen from its tip down to the ovules at its base.

Very often seeds are contained within a *capsular fruit*, which is the result of the ovaries of the flower developing into what is in effect a container for the seed. It is often easy to see the relationship between a capsule and the flower from which it is derived. Capsular fruits can take a variety of forms. The pod is one, characteristic of the pea family, the Fabaceae, where one *carpel* or division of the ovary develops into a casing, which when ripe splits open along both sides. The *siliqua*, common among the cabbage family or Brassicaceae, is similar but developed from two fused carpels, with a distinctive membrane, the *septum*, dividing the two. Sometimes the ripe

septum is quite showy, as in honesty, *Lunaria annua*. Sometimes each carpel forms a structure called a *follicle*, which splits only along one side. Follicles are nearly always compound, forming a radially symmetrical structure – *Aquilegia* and *Aconitum* are good examples.

The *capsule* is a very common form of fruit, a container for the seed which, when ripe, opens, allowing seed to be shaken out. Often the top lifts off, as in campanulas; in

others, small pores in the side allow seed out, like a pepperpot, as in poppies. Whatever the mechanism, the principle is the same: when wind and other causes of movement shake the dry seedhead stalk, the seeds are propelled out. The taller the stem, the further the seeds are likely to go.

In some cases, the fruit splits up into a number of dry structures resembling achenes; these are called *mericarps*. In the case of the wild carrot family, the Apiaceae

opposite *Asclepias speciosa* has seed capsules which split down one side to reveal relatively large seeds with silky fibres attached to carry them away on the slightest breeze.

right *Acanthus spinosus* has large seeds inside capsular fruit surrounded by the husks of what were once the structures of the flower.

Iris pseudacorus has typical iris fruit – upright capsules which split open sideways to release seeds, valued winter decoration in the bog garden or in shallow water by a pond.

Monarda punctata is a member of the mint family where seedcases are formed from the sepals of the flower. In this instance the individual heads are tightly packed into whorls robust enough to survive stormy autumn weather.

The large seeds of *Lunaria rediviva* are released when the papery outer casings of the seedcase fall away. The decorative silvery septum dividing the seedcase remains.

(also known as umbellifers, from Umbelliferae, the old name for the family), these structures look very much like seeds, and are popularly assumed to be so, but in fact are seeds with a coating derived from the flower ovary, two mericarps being derived from each ovary. In the mint family, Lamiaceae, the ovary splits into four, hence the appearance of seeds grouped in fours, all buried inside a casing derived from the ovary walls.

Grasses, members of the Poaceae (formerly the Graminae) dominate many open habitats across the world, and have become increasingly important as ornamental plants. Their flower- and seedheads are highly distinctive, a reflection of the unique floral structure which grasses possess. Each seed is encased within husks, forming the characteristic elongated body familiar from edible grains like wheat and barley. A particularly prominent feature on some grass seeds is the *awn*, an elongated structure left over from the flowerhead which can be very noticeable. Even awns of only a few millimetres long can catch the light and make a considerable visual impression; in extreme cases, such as some *Stipa* species from dry habitats in eastern Europe and central Asia, awns may grow to lengths measured in tens of centimetres. Persistent awns can generally be assumed to assist with seed dispersal, by catching the wind or by helping the seeds become attached to animals.

Burrs are seeds which carry hooks designed to catch on to animal fur and be transported a long way from the parent. The hooked structures may be derived from the fruit coat, the style or the involucre. *Berries* are fleshy, designed to attract foraging animals. They are far more common among woody plants than among herbaceous ones.

We could spend much longer looking at the botany of seedheads, but that is rather beyond the scope of a book which is basically about design and aesthetics.

Echinacea pallida is a member of the daisy family (Asteraceae) with seeds carried on an involucre – in this case, distinctively conical. Even when all the seed has fallen out, the heads still have ornamental value.

Asphodeline lutea has spherical seedpods with relatively large seeds. Large seeds are often found among plants with a pioneering strategy, as their size enables seedlings to establish better in difficult situations.

Suffice it to say that when I mention 'seedheads', I may horrify botanists by my vagueness. I use the term to refer to any structure which carries or contains seed, and in many cases is a structure containing many multiples of individual seedheads. An analogy is the way we talk of daisy 'flowers' to describe the compound flowerheads. Very often when we talk about 'seedheads', what we mean is the whole of the old *inflorescence* – the flowers and their supporting stems.

The ecology of seedheads

An autumn walk around the garden, or any area rich in wildflowers, will reveal a variety of the different types of seedhead we have been looking at. But observation will also reveal another dimension to the seedhead; different plant species produce seed in very different quantities, and quantity is often related to the size of the seed – the larger the seed, the more likely that only a few will be produced. The white-flowered woodland-edge perennial *Myrrhis odorata* has one of the heaviest seeds of the wildflower flora of northern Europe, each individual seed weighing around 0.7g. Only a relatively small number are produced, and it is possible to imagine gathering them all from a plant and spending no more than a few minutes counting the total number. But

in the case of an aster, with vast numbers of tiny seeds atop its seedheads, or a mullein with large numbers of small pods each containing a multitude of seeds, the task of counting the output of a single plant seems more like the labour of a botanical Hercules.

There is a fundamental trade-off going on here. Plants with large seeds are those which provide the embryo plant within each seed with plenty of nutrients to help it through its germination, so these plants are making a considerable investment in the survival of a relatively small number of seedlings. Their seeds which land and germinate have a relatively generous leeway if the conditions are not perfect, as their reserves will see them through the time it takes their young roots and seed leaves to access nutrients and light. On the other hand, plants which produce masses of small seeds are providing them with very little in the way of nutrient supplies, but instead make up for this in quantity. Their seedlings will be more vulnerable if they land on a site that is less than ideal, but there are so many more of them that this does not matter so much.

Plants have a variety of different survival strategies. Among these is the so-called 'ruderal' strategy, whereby plants are adapted to spread rapidly into unoccupied space, proceeding to flower and seed within a relatively short space of time. 'Live fast and die young' could be their motto. The plants which do this tend to be short-lived opportunists, trading off a brief lifespan against the production of large quantities of seed. Usually this seed is smaller rather than larger. Ruderal plants – sometimes called 'pioneer species' – put more of their energy into seed production than longer-lived plants

SEEDHEADS IN THE GARDEN

The seedheads of opium poppy, *Papaver somniferum*, among the flowers of *Gypsophila paniculata*. The seed is released through small holes near the top as the poppy head is shaken by the wind or passing animals.

because the seed is their primary means of ensuring the continuation of their genes. (Other plant species which produce less seed may prefer to put energy into structure, such as woody or semi-woody stems, or storage organs like fleshy roots or bulbs.) So, it is not surprising that a large number of ruderal species have particularly impressive seedheads; after all, the distribution of seed is more important to the survival of their genes than the survival of the individual plant.

Ruderals tend to be plants of disturbed habitats or particularly stressful ones, where the long-term survival of individual plants is unlikely and where the survival of genes can be guaranteed only through seed. They include annuals which complete their lifespan within one year, biennials within two, and short-lived perennials which survive for five years or less. They all tend to flower and set seed profusely, their seed being their species' long-term survival strategy. Ruderal seed often accumulates in soil where it can lie dormant for many years, eventually springing to life when conditions suitable for germination occur. Habitats which include many ruderal species are often found in Mediterranean or semi-desert climate zones, or in coastal areas. Agricultural land or waste ground always has high concentrations of ruderals, whatever the climate zone.

The soil of habitats with large numbers of ruderals is likely to have what ecologists call a large 'seed bank' of buried seeds.

These lie waiting for some chance event that will allow them to germinate – it could be disturbance which brings them to the soil surface, or the onset of rain. Many ruderal seeds last for decades; some, such as poppies, for centuries. In dry-climate zones it may be only once every few years that conditions favour germination – leading to the spectacular 'flowering of the desert', observed when vast numbers of annuals flower after heavy rains. Woodland-edge habitats where fallen trees let in light support more limited but often visually striking ruderal populations, as can be appreciated by the mass-flowering of foxgloves (*Digitalis purpurea*) in the years after tree felling. Many garden weeds are ruderals, taking advantage of the excellent opportunities provided by traditional horticultural practices – bare soil and frequent disturbance.

Among ruderals, biennials in particular tend to have physically strong and prominent seedheads. They put all the energies of their two years of photosynthesis into one spectacular production, a seedhead which tends to be tall (to ensure good distribution) and tough (to be able to withstand winter storms and so potentially shake out its seeds gradually over many months). Not surprisingly, we tend to admire the visual qualities of such plants.

Ruderal plants tend to be found concentrated in particular floral families. The Apiaceae (generally referred to as the umbellifers) is one such. The vast majority of its temperate-zone members are biennial, germinating in one year, overwintering as a nutrient-packed fleshy root, and then flowering, seeding and dying in the

following year. Both carrot and parsnip are members. Umbellifers, as their name suggests, tend to have lots of tiny flowers massed into umbels – rounded, often plate-like inflorescences. Their seeds are rarely small, and quite often large, and so are produced in relatively small quantities. Umbellifers are rarely colourful and so have tended to be ignored by gardeners, but they have considerable structural interest, which is at last being valued more widely by contemporary designers.

Another family with a great number of visually exciting seedheads is the Scrophulariaceae, which includes many well-known genera such as the foxgloves (*Digitalis*) and mulleins (*Verbascum*). Many of these are notable for having strongly upright inflorescences in the form of spikes or spires (or, speaking botanically, racemes). The physical strength of these seedheads and their supporting stems makes them particularly useful in gardens. A great many are very profuse seeders, producing vast amounts of very small seed, which means that in garden they often reappear as seedlings. Superficially similar in flower structure to members of this family are the Lamiaceae, the mint family. Although having a greater tendency towards being long-lived, many of these too have quite robust seedheads, making them useful for winter design effects.

Many other herbaceous plants have a survival strategy which could be described as 'competitive' – that is to say, they fight for space by growing vigorously to smother competition or to pre-empt it. Others, the competitive-ruderals, have an intermediate strategy. Many of these have distinctive

seedheads, but being longer-lived, these plants tend to set less store on surviving only through the genes in their seeds, and so their physically weaker seedheads are less likely to survive the winter. Among them the Asteraceae are worth mentioning for the very large number of species with moderately interesting and durable seedheads and the important role which they play in many open habitats. The Liliaceae are also worth mentioning for similar reasons, although they are ecologically far less dominant in the habitats where they occur.

Grasses, or the Poaceae, play an overwhelmingly dominant role in many open habitats in cool temperate climates and in seasonally moist warmer ones. Their seedheads are often visually distinctive, and their physically robust nature, which makes them so valuable in the garden, is a function of the fact that they tend to invest more energy in the construction of their stems than many non-grasses. This combination of characteristics makes them eminently suitable for plantings with winter-long interest.

left *Dipsacus fullonum*, the teasel, is a well-known biennial wildflower whose heads have long been used, and indeed are still used industrially, for finishing cloth. In damp weather seed can be so impatient to get going that it can even germinate while still in the head – as here.

opposite Grasses in the garden of Piet and Anja Oudolf at Hummelo in the Netherlands. *Panicum virgatum* 'Rehbraun' at the rear, *Pennisetum alopecuroides* 'Cassian's Choice' at lower left, and *Sporobolus heterolepis* at lower right. Siting larger grasses to catch low-angled winter sunlight is crucial. A variety of other flowering perennial seedheads is effectively highlighted against the grasses.

Designing with Seedheads

Seedheads rarely have much to offer in the way of colour, at least in comparison with flowers or even foliage. Instead, their aesthetic qualities are best appreciated through their form, so it is useful to begin with some basic categories and concepts which will help our approach to understanding and using the beauty of seedheads in the garden.

A number of basic shapes appear and reappear in the world of the seedhead. To a large extent they reflect the shape of the inflorescence from which they are derived. The following classification of shapes owes much to Piet Oudolf.

Single seeds Occasionally, individual seeds or their immediate supporting structures are large enough to make a visual impact, as with the annual *Atriplex hortensis* var. *rubra*, whose large grain-like heads are clearly visible, or the bunches of winged seeds of maples. All types of grasses fall into this category.

Single heads and pods Some individual seedheads are large enough to dominate our impression of a plant, whether they are single or in bunches. The big upright pointed cases of many members of the

Apocynaceae, such as *Asclepias*, or the bean-like pods of the Fabaceae are good examples. Such seedheads have a strong and somewhat definite look about them and tend to be visually arresting. Lighter, feathery seedheads make a good visual contrast.

Spikes Although plants which carry their flowers and seedheads on tall stems to form spikes or spires are relatively few, they are invaluable for structural effect, particularly during winter. They include many Scrophulariaceae such as verbascums. The repetition of spikes across a space can be one of the most visually arresting features in perennial planting. Many seedheads form less immediately noticeable spikes, or at least upright heads. While these tend to have less impact, they are useful for the sense of structure they create.

Umbels Such seedheads are gathered into rounded structures, which can vary from practically flat-topped in the case of *Achillea filipendulina* to very rounded in the case of *Angelica gigas*. The flatter ones (as most are) contrast effectively with spires, with the horizontal balancing the vertical. Massed

above left The stiff seedheads of foxgloves stand the winter well. All are short-lived plants of woodland-edge and other rapidly changing habitats, where the spread of taller plants such as shrubs and young trees will rapidly eliminate good growing conditions for them – so their only hope of long-term survival is by spreading themselves around through seeding. This is *Digitalis grandiflora*, which has yellow flowers in early summer.

left *Verbascum lychnitis* has white flowers in early summer, followed by tall, branched seedheads. Verbascums are plants of habitats where soil disturbance is common, such as slopes or waste ground, or where light soil and drought combine to limit the development of a more long-lived plant canopy.

opposite *Pennisetum alopecuroides* 'Cassian's Choice' has fluffy and rather tactile flower- and seedheads, and is decorative for much of the late-summer and autumn period. Pennisetums are distinctive for having flowers and seeds arranged in tightly packed spikes.

top left Plants such as this *Sanguisorba officinalis*, whose seedheads form tight buttons, are especially effective in creating points of definition against looser and lighter backgrounds.

top right From mid-autumn on, the seedheads of *Miscanthus sinensis* 'Juli' turn a silvery-grey. Many grasses have flower- and seedheads in loose, multi-branched structures known as panicles.

above The ornamental garlics or alliums have seedheads in umbels or, in the case of one group of west Asian semi-desert species, in globes. This is *Allium hollandicum*.

opposite Umbellifers gain their name from the umbel-shaped flower- and seedheads characteristic of the family. This is *Angelica sylvestris* 'Vicar's Mead'.

umbels, as with *Sedum spectabile* hybrids or *Achillea* hybrids, can be striking, but lack the impact of massed spikes.

Globes. Relatively few seedheads form globes, but the ones that do are invaluable, loved by both gardeners and flower-arrangers. We seem to take particular delight in those that form near-perfect spheres, such as certain alliums.

Panicles Loose structures with seedheads in multi-branched heads are often not particularly dramatic unless either launched skywards on tall stems or particularly finely feathery, as with some grasses. In many cases they may have a decorative

vagueness, and sometimes even a see-through quality, as with many cultivars of the grass *Molinia caerulea*.

Buttons Those members of the Asteraceae and others which have their flowers and then their seeds closely packed into tight heads, such as *Centaurea*, are often useful for contrasting with wispy panicles. Tight points of definition are especially useful in wildflower meadows, as all around them tends to appear loose and chaotic.

Whorls Whorls of seedheads arranged around an upright stem give an impression of order and design, and can be very effective if repeated across a space.

The more tightly the individual seedheads are packed, the greater the feeling of definition.

Seedheads in the late-season garden

Seedheads play a crucial role in the late-autumn and winter garden, and here we look at the role they can play in planting design for these times of year. But before we proceed, it is quite instructive to think about how we actually look at gardens, and in particular to consider the comparative

distances between us, the viewer, the structures of the garden and the objects of our immediate attention.

Exploring a garden is a process which involves constant movement as you examine and appreciate its environment both at long and short ranges, and everything in between. This is reflected in how gardens are represented in garden photography: any magazine article inevitably includes some wide-angle shots which give an overall sense of the garden, some medium-range

ones which tend to focus on plant combinations or garden features, and close-ups of individual plants.

The larger-scale structures of a garden are always present in our awareness – they have to be, otherwise we would not be able to navigate our way around them. But at some times we pay much greater attention to them than at others – when we first walk into a garden, for example, or enter for the first time an area which offers a distinctly different vista. There are also those

moments when we have been examining individual plants or plant combinations quite closely, and feel the need to look up, to take a wider view. Such moments are necessary psychologically and physiologically, to rest the mind and relax eye muscles, but also to remind ourselves of where we are, and to put what we have been looking at in detail into context.

First of all, seedheads, like flowers, can be viewed in close-up. This is an opportunity to appreciate their intricacy, to see them as individuals, without any other distractions. Secondly, they can be appreciated in the garden at relatively close hand, by walking along a border, for example, where they are within two or three metres of where we stand and pause. This is a good way of seeing several together, of appreciating the interplay of different forms and colours. Lastly, they can be appreciated from afar. Seen from a distance, they can play a major part in determining and defining the overall character of a garden in autumn and winter.

Many seedheads are interesting and attractive when seen from the middle distance, but the number which make an impact over a greater distance is reduced. This is partly due to size, but also because of subtlety of colouring or lack of definition – many simply do not stand out much from a distance. Those that do create an impact at a distance are especially valuable for whole garden design rather than just as elements in a planting or simply being objects of interest. Grasses dominate the

above Not only can death be beautiful, but decay also. This poppy head has started to disintegrate, revealing the skeletal beauty of its underlying structure.

left The Piet Oudolf borders at the Royal Horticultural Society garden at Wisley in Surrey are perhaps at their most spectacular in early winter, with bold masses of grasses and flowering perennial seedheads. On the left *Glycyrrhiza yunnanensis* is highlighted against grass *Deschampsia cespitosa*. In the middle foreground are the dark umbels of a *Sedum spectabile* cultivar and on the right is *Eryngium yuccifolium*.

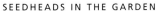

Optimizing visual impact

Individual specimens of the following plants and grasses can make a good visual impact at a distance of over 15m in winter:	When massed or loosely grouped, the following plants and grasses can make a good visual impact at a distance of over 15m in winter:
Angelica archangelica	Astilbe
Aralia	Achillea
Aster umbellatus	Digitalis ferruginea
Calamagrostis	Dipsacus fullonum
Cercis	Eremurus
Clematis	Geum triflorum
Cortaderia	Iris sibirica
Cotinus	Ligularia
Deschampsia cespitosa	Lunaria
Echium pininana	Lythrum
Eryngium pandanifolium	Matteuccia
Ferula	Panicum virgatum
Gunnera	Phlomis
Heracleum mantegazzianum	Schizachyrium
Hydrangea	Sedum
Miscanthus	Sorghastrum
Molinia	Sporobolus
Pennisetum	Verbascum
Phormium	Veronicastrum
Stipa gigantea	
Typha (larger species)	

distance category because of their size, their durability and their impact.

Placed at relatively close hand, any attractively shaped seedheads can be used to create interest. Paths which wend between plantings offer a much higher interface between plant and viewer than those which only allow us to look from afar. They also offer great opportunities for the visually disabled to get access to feel them: seedheads arguably offer greater opportunities for aesthetic stimulation for this group than do flowers.

From further away, lighting and contrast are the keys to getting the most out of seedheads. Very light and very dark

combinations will be much more striking at a distance than those where there is little contrast, as will strong contrasts of form. Grasses, which tend to have paler stems than herbaceous plants, are particularly valuable for providing a pale counterpoint to darker stems. Alternations between dark and pale can be very striking, such as between the dark brown *Veronicastrum virginicum* and the pale frothy heads of the grass *Deschampsia cespitosa*. Contrast in form is also useful for highlighting the qualities of each and generating a sense of creative tension. Here clear definition against lack of definition is the key issue – exploring how the hard-edged and clearly

defined can contrast with the soft and vague. Many grasses have a very soft, wispy quality, such as the deschampsia just mentioned, as do some leafy plants such as *Gypsophila altissima*. This is most effective when used as a backdrop for hard, tightly defined shapes such as those of many mint-family plants (Lamiaceae) like *Monarda* and *Phlomis*. A sense of mass against light and feathery can also be developed, such as between the solid, heavy feel of clumps of *Sedum spectabile* and other similar species against light and soft-looking grasses.

The play of light on seedheads is particularly important for the effect that they make at a distance. In winter nearly all seedheads and associated dead plant material have a brown or fawn tone, the odd yellow standing out as the brightest colour. Light is essential for bringing out subtleties which cannot otherwise be appreciated, such as tones of pink, red and violet. Winter sunshine is low and has a higher proportion of warm-toned red and yellow light than the higher sun of summer – which fortuitously brings out the best of the tones in this colour range that seedheads tend to exhibit. Although combinations of pale tones do not generally stand out, such warm light can in some circumstances pick out and highlight subtle differences; a good example is the dull reds of the grass *Schizachyrium scoparium* and the light grey stems of the subshrub *Perovskia atriplicifolia*.

The angle of winter sunlight that hits the garden varies according to latitude. At lower latitudes in temperate and Mediterranean-climate regions, winter sunlight is strong relative to that at higher

above Dark definition against lightness and looseness: *Phlomis tuberosa* and *Deschampsia cespitosa*.

right *Cortaderia selloana* 'Sunningdale Silver' is a variety of the familiar pampas grass which, given the right location (plenty of space, big surroundings), can look magnificent, especially in strong winter sunlight.

latitudes – a strength often combined with a clarity of light. In these conditions landscapes can be strongly lit but at the same time bleached of colour – everything is in shades of fawn, straw and grey, the only colour being the dull, dark green of evergreens and, of course, the intense blue of the sky. As a result, our eyes become

attuned to the smallest differences, the most delicate subtleties, between colours and textures. At higher latitudes, the angle of light is lower and the day is shorter. The longer period of warmer light which results from the passage of sunlight through a considerable distance of the earth's atmosphere is ideal for illuminating seedheads and dead stems, and for highlighting the red and yellow element in them – browns, in particular, are no longer just brown, but tan-browns, russet browns, yellow-shot browns. However, the low angle and short total diurnal duration of light arriving in the garden can severely limit what gets lit up and for how long. Plant positioning then is crucial – seedheads to be appreciated at a distance need placing where the sun will hit them for as long as possible. Tall grasses, such as some of the *Miscanthus* varieties, are particularly useful as the taller the plant, the longer it will remain in the light.

Seedheads are likely to play different roles in gardens, depending on what other plant features they are combined with – and all this depends very much on climate. Continental climates tend to have relatively short autumns, as warm summers turn rapidly to cold winters, whereas maritime climates often have long drawn-out autumnal periods. In continental climates there will be only limited opportunities for seeing flowers and seedheads together, whereas in maritime ones herbaceous border plantings can have weeks of gradual winding down, with late-flowering plants such as asters and eupatoriums hanging on bravely, producing blooms for weeks while everything around them disintegrates. There are clearly opportunities here for bringing together flowers and seedheads. Particularly effective can be combinations of some of the grasses with late-flowering perennials. The russets and silvers of the former can be very striking alongside the colours which

above Low-angled winter sunlight on the Piet Oudolf borders at Wisley.

opposite Backlighting can perform magic. This is *Agastache rugosa*, with *Monarda fistulosa* in the background.

seem to dominate autumn flowers – violets and purples and yellows. These very late-flowering perennials tend not to have very interesting seedheads, but their flowers can be effectively combined with those which have finished and gone to seed a month or so earlier, such as species and varieties of *Monarda*, *Echinacea*, *Ligularia* and so on.

Late autumn, or autumn itself in continental climates where the growing season shuts down more firmly, can be a marvellous time for combining russet colours and seedheads. The increasing warmth of late-season low sunlight is perfect for bringing out the best in tree and shrub autumn foliage colour, which can form a very strong colour theme. Seedheads are rarely colourful (although their supporting

above The silvery seedheads (or more correctly, the inner wall of disintegrated heads) of *Lunaria rediviva*, with the berry-like orange fruits of *Malus floribunda*. The dark orange lanterns in the centre are the husks which surround the berries of the herbaceous *Physalis alkekengi*.

opposite The clean, dark lines of *Lythrum salicaria* stand out against the autumnal foliage of *Euphorbia palustris*.

stems may be), but their distinctive forms are an interesting counterpoint to broad masses of background coloured foliage. Autumn colour in the herbaceous border should not be forgotten, either – its potential is often

not realized. Colour in dying herbaceous foliage tends to develop much better in continental climates (or after particularly hot summers in maritime climates) and can be very striking alongside seedheads. The yellow of *Euphorbia palustris* and of *Coreopsis tripteris* can be dramatic, and some geranium species can develop striking red tones – *Geranium wlassovianum* and *G. sanguineum* are two that come to mind. Many grasses develop good colours more readily – the yellows which the cultivars of *Molinia caerulea* tend to turn are particularly dramatic, long-lasting and predictable.

Berries and fleshy fruit are very much the woody-plant counterpart of seedheads on herbaceous plants. As we shall see in the plant directory, there is some cross-over: a very few herbaceous plants have berries and a modest number of trees and shrubs have interesting dry seedheads. But berry production is largely the preserve of plants with woody stems, for a variety of reasons. Fleshy fruit is heavy and needs strong stems to support it. Since berry or fruit production is a seed-distribution strategy that depends on harvesting by birds and mammals, woody branches are a convenient support not only

for the food but also for the wildlife which comes to eat it. Berries and fruit need to advertise their presence, so not surprisingly are often brightly coloured; birds, incidentally, have better colour vision than mammals. The colours tend to be those which show up best in the lower wavelengths of winter sunlight – reds, oranges and yellows.

Berries can form an interesting pairing with seedheads in the winter garden. They are almost always the brightest aspect of a winter garden, bringing colour to sombre and bleached landscapes, yet never having the intricate form of seedheads or their potential for interesting silhouettes or shadows. They are nearly always to be found higher up, and so are more likely to dominate the middle or far distance in our view of a garden. We have already seen how some seedheads, notably grasses, dominate the long to medium distance, whereas others, chiefly those of non-grassy herbaceous plants, need to be seen at close range to be appreciated. Berry-bearing woody plants are clearly a part of the longer-range spectacle.

A limited number of herbaceous plants produce berries. They are the jokers in the pack, surprises, almost like nature playing a trick. The bright orange-red of arum berries or of the orange-coated seeds which peep out of the seedpods of *Iris foetidissima* are all the more dramatic for being the only points of such colour among the fawns, browns and yellows of the late autumn or

The cold but beautiful world of grasses and perennials after a hoar frost: *Calamagrostis* x *acutiflora* 'Karl Foerster' at rear, *Panicum virgatum* at lower right and *Helenium* varieties at lower left.

Echinacea pallida dusted with frost. Larger seeds are particularly good as winter food sources for many smaller birds.

winter border. They are 'down there', not hanging in mid-air on branches where we expect to seem them, which makes them objects of curiosity – an element of garden aesthetics which has always been important, but which has been somewhat forgotten.

Many seedheads are very effective when seen in silhouette, especially those of darker colouring. Only a few are tall enough to be seen against the sky, except when on a slope where it is possible to look up at them. The alternative is to position plants against walls where the sun can strike them and cast shadows. Shadows appear differently depending upon the colour, and the texture, of the surface they are cast on. At higher latitudes, warm-coloured surfaces

The steppe area at Lady Farm in hoar frost, with *Stipa gigantea* particularly prominent. Among the other grasses are several *Miscanthus* cultivars (the larger ones with fawn stems) and *Stipa tenuissima* (small, with stems bending over).

– yellow ochre, mustard, terracotta – are most effective, as the wavelengths of light available in autumn and winter tend to be biased towards these tones. At latitudes where winter sunlight is particularly strong and less warm, a wider range of colours can be experimented with.

Snow and frost are what really bring out the best in seedheads. Hoar frost, which coats every single edge with a rime of crystals creates utterly magical effects, transforming the most mundane of scenes into a wonderland. Its power to make us look anew at just about any plant material is considerable, rather like that of a hallucinatory drug. Such conditions are a good opportunity to get anyone who has never looked at seedheads hooked on their visual possibilities. Snow is different, cruder in many ways, as it blankets, obscures and obfuscates. A very heavy snowfall is capable of more or less crushing all herbaceous growth in a garden. Lighter falls can blanket the ground but leave stronger and more firmly upright seedheads standing, to be emphasized against the pure white background. Less robust seedheads are physically crushed, or at least weighed down; lighter-coloured ones can fade into the background, but stronger ones appear even stronger, darker ones even darker. Seedheads on sturdy stalks are at their best a day or two after a snowfall, when the fine layer of snow which settled on every surface has fallen off, leaving snow only on the ground and other level surfaces. Now the upright stems can stand proud, their colour and texture an absolute contrast to all around them. Flowering perennials tend to be more effective at this time than grasses, as they are more likely to have prominent darker stems. Very tall and strong plants such as the larger eupatoriums or vernonias are especially striking.

Frost in a garden adds infinite levels of complexity, as every little detail is enhanced and magnified, whereas snow simplifies and emphasizes only the architectural or that with enough mass to stand out. But what about mist and fog? In the obscurity imposed on a garden landscape by such weather conditions, it is only the larger and more imposing seedheads which have any hope of being seen. They are made visible in a way which can be very dramatic, as mist has the effect of magnifying tall objects so that they have the appearance of looming over us. Large umbellifers such as *Angelica archangelica* can seem like fantastical extraterrestrial beings; verbascum

species, foxgloves (*Digitalis ferruginea* especially) and anything else with a tall narrow seedhead becomes anthropomorphic. *Echium pininana* with its three-metre-plus spires is the most dramatic and gothic in atmosphere of all. Given that this frost-tender species does best in coastal gardens where fog is common, this aspect of the plant's aesthetic is one which is particularly relevant.

Seedheads in natural and formal-style gardens

The seedhead aesthetic is, as we have seen, one which is very much a part of the move towards the appreciation of wilder and less controlled plantings. But this should not dissuade those who like (or who work with) more formal plantings from experimenting with using them too. They will probably find the use of monocultural blocks of planting more to their taste than combinations of many different heavily intermingled species. Physically robust seedheads which last a long time would be more appropriate for such a planting style, too. Although Piet Oudolf is not known for his formal approach to planting, he has sometimes explored a real narrowing down of his usual plant palette and has produced some striking results. In particular he has on a number of occasions (for instance, at Bury Court in Hampshire, England) used the grass *Deschampsia cespitosa* in blocks to create a stylized meadow effect, a soft romantic haze

The formality of these hedges (at Piet and Anja Oudolf's garden) is counterbalanced by the looseness of perennials: *Amsonia salicifolia* with yellow autumn colour, *Eupatorium cannabinum*, *Verbena hastata* and *Rudbeckia maxima*.

of golden-straw-coloured seedheads. Occasional flowering perennials with strong form (such as *Digitalis ferruginea* and *Trifolium rubens*) make an appearance to act as a contrast. The US designer Topher Delaney has used *Stipa tenuissima* in some gardens in California to similar effect. There are probably many other species which could be used – it is still early days for ornamental grasses in horticulture.

An intermediate style of planting design can be seen in the work of James van Sweden and Wolfgang Oehme in the eastern United States. Here there is none of the formality and geometry associated with the garden style of 'old Europe', but a clear sense of order and control is achieved through the use of distinct groupings of plants, which may number from a cluster of individuals through to large blocks. The repetition of the same shape creates a powerful impression, one which has been particularly successful in the many corporate or public landscapes which the partnership have designed. Grasses have played a prominent role in their work, for instance varieties of *Pennisetum*, which create a very soft, meadowy look when planted *en masse*, or *Calamagrostis* x *acutiflora* 'Stricta', which has a more orderly look as a result of the firm, upright character of the flower- and seedheads. Oehme–van Sweden plantings have enough wild character (largely through the use of the grasses) to evoke prairie and other wild habitats, but

Formality is not just for woody plants. Here at Bury Court, a Piet Oudolf garden in southern England, a knob of box is ringed with *Molinia caerulea* 'Poul Petersen'. In the background is a 'meadow' of *Deschampsia cespitosa* 'Goldtau'.

above Cultivars of *Sedum spectabile* at Sticky Wicket, Dorset, England.

left *Calamagrostis* x *acutiflora* 'Karl Foerster' flowers early, and its seedheads are formed by midsummer. Here it makes a structural centrepiece for a border including an *Acanthus spinosus* (immediately in front of it) and *Panicum virgatum* (in the foreground).

enough of a sense of order to appeal to a public which expects gardens and landscapes to look tidy and under control.

The larger the group of individuals of a single variety that is used, the more important it becomes for that variety to have a long season of interest. A key part of the success of Oehme–van Sweden Associates has been the extensive trialling of plants by Wolfgang Oehme. Particular favourites are, not surprisingly, those which never have an 'off day'; in many cases this includes having good seedheads. *Sedum spectabile* and its hybrids are a good example, as their flowers fade gracefully before turning to tough, umbel-shaped heads composed of masses of tiny seed capsules. It could be said that while frosted gardens helped put Piet Oudolf on the map, snow has done the same for Oehme–van Sweden gardens.

For those who work with the wild look, it is important to get just the right degree of wildness. Autumn and winter can be a chaotic time in the garden, especially one dominated by herbaceous plants – stems falling this way and that, some plants

collapsing into a soggy mass with the first frost, a few raggedy asters still bravely flowering whatever the weather is doing. The use of species with physically strong stems, persistent seedheads and clear, definite shapes all helps to create winter pictures of order. They will give structure and backbone to scenes of frost- and wind-induced dishevelment, especially if scattered liberally through a planting. Many of the best of these, for good reasons of ecology, as we have seen, are those which tend to

be short-lived and free with their seed, such as teasels, mulleins and foxgloves. The fact that some may be a little too eager to spread themselves around through seeding should be regarded as a small price to pay for having them as a continuing presence in the garden.

A key issue in contemporary planting design is that of the degree of intermingling. Conventionally, herbaceous plants have been grown in clumps of several individuals of the same variety. Some

An overview of borders at Hermannshof in autumn, with a number of *Miscanthus* varieties at the point of transition between flower and seed.

more naturalistic planting schemes have begun to experiment with intermingling – which is what happens in nature. What one thinks of the results is very much a matter of subjective and personal opinion. Blocks of identical plants are undeniably particularly effective at seedhead time, at least for some; shapes which tend to

reinforce each other can be striking –
massed spires of *Digitalis* or *Veronicastrum*,
or repeated bobbles of *Phlomis* or *Monarda*.
In other cases a chaotic variety of different
shapes can look remarkably good – it was
photographs of parsnips and carrots gone
to seed alongside leeks and opium poppies
which helped bring fame to Henk
Gerritsen's Priona garden in the eastern
Netherlands. Such an approach to the
vegetable garden – letting it all go to seed –
can be taken as a something of an artistic
statement, for many vegetables are actually
quite good-looking in their rarely seen or
appreciated seeding phase.

The use of seedheads in gardens and
public landscapes has been particularly
associated with the naturalistic planting
style that developed in the Netherlands and
Germany from the 1970s on, itself the
result of a much longer process of gestation
reaching back to the end of the nineteenth
century. In Germany the garden-festival
movement has played a major role in
promoting a style of planting based on
a nature-inspired aesthetic and a strong
ecological bias in plant selection. Areas of
derelict land, usually once occupied by
manufacturing or extractive industries or
the military, are turned into summer-long
garden festivals in which naturalistic
perennial planting plays a big part.
When the festival is over, much of the
infrastructure and planting is left to become
the core of a public park. In many cases

Grass seedheads at Sticky Wicket, a garden in
Dorset, England, which has also experimented
with naturalistic planting. *Hordeum jubatum* is
in the centre, while the very fine texture is
Agrostis nebulosa. The violet flowers are
Verbena bonariensis.

the winter aspect of these plantings is particularly effective, and offers an excellent opportunity to see perennials *en masse*. Those species which self-sow and repeat themselves across large areas, such as *Eryngium giganteum* and mulleins, can make a particularly striking effect.

On a somewhat more intimate scale is the Hermannshof garden at Weinheim in Germany, founded in 1983 by the Freudenberg company as a public garden with a strong educational emphasis. Each individual planting is much smaller than in the festival landscapes, and the whole setting much less expansive. It is a place in which it is possible to get a good idea of an ecologically based planting scheme on a more realistically domestic scale – including, of course, the winter seedhead aspect.

Of the variety of habitat-inspired plantings in the garden-festival sites, the one which has made the most impact has arguably been the 'steppe', a combination of drought-tolerant species inspired by the areas of dry grassland which are typical of certain parts of central Europe, and which become a major landscape element in Ukraine. Steppe plants have to grow rapidly in spring and early summer when there is good available moisture, and be prepared for a long summer drought. A characteristic of many of them is robust and distinctive seedheads: the upright stems of various mint-family species with seed capsules grouped into tight whorls at regular intervals up the stem, lily-family members such as *Asphodeline* species with seedheads in spikes, and a huge variety of grasses. Because the climate is dry, growth tends to be reduced and often has a tougher quality

about it than that of plants in lusher environments. In winter there is less likelihood that these species will collapse in the autumn rain; instead, they carry on looking good and architectural for many months.

Somewhat indirectly, the steppe plantings in German parks have inspired Lady Farm, a garden in the south-west of England. The garden has attracted a lot of interest for its firmly contemporary design and its winter interest – largely achieved through grasses. The most striking part of the site is a 'steppe' planting on a hill, with grasses such as cultivars of *Miscanthus* and *Molinia* – and the much smaller and very fine *Stipa tenuissima* – repeating over the whole area. The whole scene is highly effective even in grey winter weather, a result of the repetition of a limited number of distinct forms.

In parts of its geographical range, steppe, and the short-grass prairie of the Great Plains, its North American equivalent, tends to grade into the Mediterranean climate zone. Here, human activities have massively reduced the spread of the original plant cover – which was often largely forest – to a lower, shrubby vegetation. In more open areas a sparse flora is dominated by annuals, at least visually. Indeed, the majority of the annual species in cultivation are from the Mediterranean area or California, and there are many more whose garden potential is yet to be realized. Annuals can germinate at the start of the mild wet winter, grow

Sometimes it is the sheer size of prairie perennials which gives their main appeal. These are the 2.5m stems of *Eupatorium purpureum* subsp. *maculatum* 'Atropurpureum' in frost.

through it, and then flower and seed in the early summer. As with all ruderals, the seedhead is considerably more important to the future survival of the species than in longer-lived plants, so, not surprisingly, a great many of these Mediterranean-zone annuals have striking seedheads. Examples include poppies (*Papaver* species), love-in-a-mist (*Nigella damascena*) and quaking grass (*Briza maxima*), to name but three cottage-garden favourites.

In North America, the discovery of the prairie as a wildflower habitat of enormous richness and beauty has inspired a new generation of gardeners and ecologists to work with it, as a planting for private gardens and public and corporate landscapes. The autumn and winter aspect offers plenty of variety of seedheads, although the aesthetic value will depend very much on the particular mix of species. The winter foliage colour of prairie plants can also be of great visual interest. 'Prairie' plantings also have a future in Europe, where the term has begun to be applied to naturalistic plantings which rely for their impact on large perennials, usually on fertile soils, as the use of strong-growing plant species which can tolerate weed competition helps to contribute towards minimizing maintenance requirements. Visually interesting seedheads can be an important part of the whole prairie aesthetic, whether the prairie is an 'ecologically correct' one in the American Midwest, or a more relaxed border of robust perennials elsewhere.

'Drumstick' allium heads in midsummer with *Echinacea purpurea*.

European wildflower meadow arguably has less seedhead interest than steppe or prairie. The number of species with good persistent seedheads on stems which are tall enough to make them stand out is relatively small. Central and south-eastern European floras probably offer the best range; those of north and west Europe the least. In addition, meadow in north-western regions tends to become a soggy, lumpy mass as the long autumn's rain and wind endlessly pummel grasses and flowering plants.

Piet Oudolf's work has brought the winter aspect of perennials to a much wider public – partly through simply using plants with good lasting seedheads and not cutting them down until the end of the winter, but also through his photographic documentation of his own projects – which well illustrates the adage that a product is only as good as its marketing. Illustrations of his gardens during winter sparked a minor fashion in winter seedhead shots – preferably in hoar frost. It was soon pointed out that hoar frost is comparatively rare in many climate zones. The exquisite scenes portrayed in books and magazines will only occur, in the first place, if severe autumn wind and rain have not bashed the perennials into a brown pulp, and, in the second, if and when there is a hoar frost. Nevertheless, the point that seedheads can be beautiful had been made, and that any case, when there is little else to admire in the garden in the dreary early winter period, you might prefer to look at brown seedheads than bare earth.

The Oudolf approach to designing with perennials, and with perennials 'out of season' in particular, has struck a chord with the gardening public, because it provides a middle way between the two positions which have tended to define discussions about garden design for the last few centuries: the formal and the informal or nature-inspired. The naturalistic drifts of perennials which feature in German garden-festival parks or at Lady Farm look fantastic, but it could be argued that this is partly a result of the scale on which they are made. In addition, there is the feeling that the majority of the garden-appreciating public does like rather more architectural structure than this very naturalistic and structureless style can offer. Oudolf's masses of seedheads and dead stems are balanced by blocks of geometrically trimmed evergreens and architectural garden layouts. Such a balancing of Bacchus and Apollo is one which is perhaps the most widely appreciated approach to garden making, which brings us back to the beginning of this particular discussion.

Seedheads in the summer garden

Most seedheads are produced in autumn, and we have so far considered them very much in the context of the late-season garden. But some early-flowering perennials produce seedheads which ripen by midsummer, so that they can be a feature of summer planting combinations. On a small scale, the feathery bobbles of pulsatillas can make a striking feature in the rock garden or in other combinations of low-growing plants. Clematis is, somewhat surprisingly, a relation, as can readily be appreciated by looking at the form of the seedhead. Early-flowering clematis species, such as *C. alpina*, *C. macropetala*,

Artist and 'hortisculpturalist' Stella Carr and colleague Anna Douglas at work spray-painting verbascum seedheads. The colours used are chosen to reflect the vibrancy of late-autumn russet tones but also a certain earthiness – so the results are surprisingly subtle. Others may choose more 'shocking' or consciously artificial colours.

C. koreana and their hybrids, have particularly good seedheads which form glistening balls of fluff by midsummer, and can make an interesting feature alongside other climbing plants or perennials.

Certain alliums have seedheads which are rated particularly highly. Large 'drumstick' heads can be very striking in borders of flowering perennials, their sere tones and appearance an effective contrast as well as a foretaste of the autumn to come.

Seedheads and wildlife

Seeds are packed with carbohydrates and proteins and as such make an excellent source of food for wildlife in winter. Indeed, the evolutionary development of the larger seeds and of nuts can be seen as a rather expensive means of achieving effective dispersal – expensive, that is, in terms of the plants' resource management. But this

Verbascums add a statuesque presence to autumn and winter borders and are generally weatherproof.

is another example of the trade-offs with which ecology is filled – if a plant makes its seeds an attractive food source for animals, then it will get plenty of attention, and as the seeds are eaten, plenty will be scattered and hence spread.

Seedheads are, not surprisingly, a good way of catering for wildlife, of helping to provide small mammals and birds with resources at a time of year when other food may be scarce. Those interested in bird-watching may indeed want to plant seed-bearing plants deliberately where they may be easily viewed from the house. It is not just the seed which is a food source, however; many herbaceous plants play host to insect larvae which hatch from eggs laid in the flowers and which then feed on the seeds as they grow. During winter many of these may go into their chrysalis stage, to emerge as adults in spring. Their existence means that many insect-eating birds will have a winter food source too.

In some regions it is even possible to

buy seed mixes of perennials especially for the production of winter seed for birds. In addition, it is possible to grow seed crops which provide both ornament and plentiful seed for birds: *Amaranthus* and millet (*Panicum miliaceum*) are the best.

Other purposes for seedheads

Seedheads, especially those which need to be seen at close range to be appreciated, are ideal for winter and permanent floral arrangements. Their lifespan is, however, inevitably limited by how long they last before becoming covered in dust – which is generally impossible to clean off. Seedheads which are to be used in such arrangements need to be picked when they are in peak condition, and then carefully dried by hanging them up in a warm dry place.

If the seed itself is needed, either for propagation, or for food in the case of grain crops like *Amaranthus*, then the heads should be cut and dried upside down in heavy paper bags. The seed will fall to the bottom of the bag as the heads dry.

It is common practice to spray-paint seedheads for use in winter floral art, but there is no reason why this cannot also be done in the garden. After all, the subtle browns and fawns of winter can become a bit dull after a while. The possibilities for a new form of winter garden art are considerable!

Cultivation

In growing plants for good seedheads we are dealing with a range of species which are well known and established in cultivation, and for the most part are unremarkable in their cultural needs. One issue that does arise concerns the short-lived nature of many good seedhead plants and their tendency to self-sow. Another is to do with the clearing away of seedheads when they have come to the end of their useful life.

Nigella damascena has particularly intriguing-looking seedheads, illustrating the surprising beauty revealed by the autumn garden. These heads can also be dried for use in winter flower arrangements.

Annuals

These are plants which can really only be propagated by seed, which usually germinates very readily. All need to be kept growing fast, without the check to growth which transplantation causes, and should either be sown where they are to flower or started off in pots. 'Hardy annuals' are those, such as *Nigella*, which can be sown directly in the ground where they are to grow and flower. 'Half-hardy annuals' need warm conditions to germinate, and in cooler climates it is the usual practice to start them off in pots inside and plant them out after the danger from late frosts is past – *Amaranthus* species are a good example.

Generally speaking, the lighter the soil, the more readily annuals (and indeed other plants) will germinate. Customary practice has been to sow hardy annuals in blocks of one variety each, but recent developments in seed mixes have meant that increasingly annuals are grown as blended combinations of up to a dozen species for a meadow-type effect. The soil needs to be reduced to a fine tilth for seed sowing, and for best results (a long flowering season especially) some addition of nutrients in the form of a balanced fertilizer is beneficial. Sowing in rows is advisable on sites where it is known that weeds are a problem – this makes hoeing off unwanted seedlings easier.

A more naturalistic effect is created where a mixture of seeds is broadcast-sown and then raked in.

Biennials

Biennials, too, germinate rapidly and can be sown where they are to flower, but it is more usual to start them off in seed trays or pots or a nursery bed and transplant them as young plants into their final positions. If young plants are being transplanted into borders of established perennials and shrubs, care must be taken to ensure that they are not overwhelmed by the existing residents, and that they can be easily located by the gardener during their first few months in the border when they are at their most vulnerable. The common-sense way of doing this is to group them in small clusters – in many cases they will be most visually effective this way, anyway. In years to come they will most likely spread themselves through the border, so developing a more spontaneous and natural-looking distribution.

The unripe seedhead of *Angelica gigas*. This is a biennial which, unfortunately, is more reluctant to self-sow than many. To ensure its continued presence in the garden, the gardener may need to intervene: save seed and sow half of it one year and the rest the next.

Self-sowing

Since many good seedhead plants are short-lived ruderals which depend upon a rapid turnover of individuals to preserve the species, there is a tendency for them to be effective self-sowers. Garden plants which tend to self-sow generally produce large quantities of seed, which germinates freely. In many cases this is desirable, as it ensures that the plant survives in a border or other planting without too much effort on the part of the gardener. It can lead to a delightfully naturalistic distribution of plants through an area – achieving a spontaneity which would be impossible to design.
A good example of a plant which achieves this in many gardens is the silvery biennial *Eryngium giganteum*, usually known as Miss Willmott's ghost for the story of its original distribution. It was a favourite of Ellen Willmott, a wealthy and garden-obsessed lady in Edwardian England, who on visits to gardening friends would surreptitiously distribute seed around their borders, leaving a legacy of ghostly-looking plants for years to come.

Problems can occur with self-sowing, however. One is its failure, when desired plants need to be annually re-propagated in order to keep them going in the garden. Another is when self-sowing becomes too successful. Failure to self-sow could be simply an idiosyncratic mismatch between soil conditions and the particular set of conditions needed by a species for germination. As a general rule lighter soils are more favourable to the germination of a wider range of species than heavier ones. Mulches on the soil surface can also inhibit germination – after all, one of their functions is to reduce the success rate of weed seeds. Gravel mulches, though, can favour the germination of a wide range of species and yet they make weed control easier as it takes little trouble to pull seedlings out. A similar effect, in the apparent increase in germination, can be seen in the paved areas of many gardens, at least where there is no concrete underlayer.

Over-enthusiastic self-sowing is one of the occupational hazards of cultivating annuals, biennials and other ruderals. Just as it is difficult to predict whether they will self-sow at all, so it is also difficult to know in advance which might become a nuisance. Those which do can usually be easily dealt with by 'creative weeding' – that is, by hoeing off the excess when they are still small.

left *Eupatorium cannabinum* is a perennial which self-sows easily. True perennials vary enormously in their readiness to self-sow.

right *Verbascum bombyciferum*, like nearly all verbascums, self-sows very readily.

Cutting back

Conventionally, herbaceous plantings were cut back in autumn, leaving a 'tidy' but dull stretch of naked earth, dotted with short sticks and maybe the odd label. Some unimaginative folk have even been known to cut down the last asters in flower, so programmed are they to 'clean the garden up' by a certain date. Clearly, the enjoyment of seedheads is part of an aesthetic and a gardening practice which aims to avoid such extremes.

However, there are issues of tidiness. Many herbaceous plants do look chaotic in autumn, particularly in climates where heavy rain and wind can cause dead plants to collapse and become soggy. How much one puts up with this is a very personal matter – there is no 'right' time to cut back. What I always do is cut back in two stages, one in early winter, to remove all the untidy collapsed material, leaving behind the more persistent and robust plants – generally grasses and those flowering perennials which stand well, such as monardas, *Phlomis russeliana* and eupatoriums. The second cut is done in late winter, and it is important to carry this out before the first of the spring bulbs emerge. Henk Gerritsen is even experimenting with not cutting back at all! Certainly the sight of hellebores and early-flowering euphorbias emerging among dead stems looks good in clear spring sunlight, but since, at the time of writing, this is the first year of the experiment, then it remains to be seen how it will look the rest of the year.

Borders at Hermannshof with *Panicum virgatum* on the left, *Aster azureus* to its right, and a variety of other perennials. The vivid blue flower is *Salvia* 'Indigo Spires'.

Plant Directory

This list is overwhelmingly composed of herbaceous perennials, with a fair proportion of grasses. The list also includes a handful of biennials and annuals. However, a few woody plants appear too, and likewise a few herbaceous plants with berries rather than seedheads. There is method behind this apparent inconsistency. This book is about seedheads, and so it seems entirely logical to include those trees and shrubs whose seeds are borne in dry capsular fruiting bodies – that is, in seedheads. And since the focus is very much on winter interest among herbaceous plants, I hope it is not stretching our net too wide to include those very few herbaceous species which bear berries.

Plants are listed by genus; this is followed by the botanical family and a brief description of the habit and growth form of the hardy members of the genus which are relevant to our purposes. Individual species and varieties are discussed only if they have particularly notable or distinct seedhead characteristics. Very often the seedheads of all members of a genus are very similar, in which case there is no separate discussion of individual plants under the heading 'Species and varieties'. Note that I use the rather vague word 'varieties' to include the more technically correct separate categories of subspecies, hybrids, cultivars and seed strains.

In describing the growth form of herbaceous plants and grasses, the expression 'clump-forming' is frequently used; this describes a habit whereby, given time, the plant forms an extensive clump, which in theory could expand infinitely. These herbaceous plants are potentially very long-lived. Those which do not form spreading clumps are generally more likely to die out after a number of years, although exact lifespans are usually very variable, and unfortunately little researched. Unless otherwise stated, it is assumed that plants mentioned are happy growing in full sun, or very light shade, in any reasonably fertile soil with readily available moisture throughout the year.

Persistence This rating is designed to give some indication of the ability of seedheads to persist through the winter. One star is for those whose seedheads do not survive the autumn, two for those which stand at least into early winter in wetter climates, and three for those which reliably stand until the end of the winter in such climates.

Hardiness Plants' ability to withstand cold temperatures is, like size, a variable and often inexact factor: this is an area where broad indications of hardiness are more helpful than exact measurements. Conventionally, hardiness is rated by a system devised by the USDA (United States Department of Agriculture) to cover the immense range of climatic variations encountered on the North American continent.

Most of Britain, Ireland, France and the Netherlands falls into Z8–9, with coastal, western and sheltered urban areas in Z9. Most of Germany and Denmark is Z7–8. Elsewhere in Europe, altitude and proximity to the sea are the main factors in producing a more regionally complex picture. As an experienced gardener knows, temperature is only one element in determining how plants will respond to winter weather, with air humidity, soil moisture content, wind and other factors playing a part.

Plants are accorded a zone number indicating the coldest zone in which the plant can be relied upon to be hardy. Where a span is shown, for example Z4–6, this indicates a range of minima to be found in a genus. I must confess to a great deal of scepticism about the practical operation of this system, as in several cases – or in particularly favourable microclimates – I am sure species are hardier than is suggested. In addition, different reference books can disagree. Where no 'Z' number is given, I have found no reliable information.

Size

Precise dimensions achieved with ruler or tape measure are not the aim: these figures are intended to give broad general indications of the relative bulk of the plants discussed.

Herbaceous plants and grasses	Shrubs
low up to 15cm (6in) high	*sub-shrubs* (with densely
small 15 to 30cm (6in to 1ft)	twiggy habit, and evergreen
medium 30cm to 1m (1 to 3ft)	foliage) up to 1m (3ft)
large 1 to 1.8m (3 to 6ft)	*small* 1 to 2m (3 to 6ft)
very large 1.5m (5ft) and over	*medium* 2 to 3m (6 to 9ft)
	large 3m and over (9ft and over)

Zones

Range of average annual minimum temperatures for zones cited in this book:

	Celsius		Fahrenheit		
Z2	−45	to −40°C	−50	to	−40°F
Z3	−40	to −35°C	−40	to	−30°F
Z4	−35	to −29°C	−30	to	−20°F
Z5	−29	to −23°C	−20	to	−10°F
Z6	−23	to −18°C	−10	to	0°F
Z7	−18	to −12°C	0	to	10°F
Z8	−12	to −7°C	10	to	20°F
Z9	−7	to −1°C	20	to	30°F

Acaena

Acaena

ROSACEAE

Size and growth form Low perennial with persistent semi-woody growth. Rapidly spreading.

Persistence ❉ ❉

Enthusiastically running New Zealand perennials with very distinctive burr-like seedheads and often interestingly coloured foliage – greys and bronzes. Evergreen, at least in milder winter climates, the pinnate leaves densely clothe tough and wiry stems which run horizontally, rooting as they go. The burrs are sometimes reported as being troublesome to cats and smaller dogs. Potentially very invasive in coastal regions.

Species and varieties A. 'Blue Haze' has blue-grey foliage as a background to pinky red burrs; *A. caesiiglauca* has similar foliage with dark red burrs; *A. novae-zelandiae* has green leaves and red burrs. *A. microphylla* 'Kupferteppich' ('Copper Carpet') is the most decorative with tiny bronzy leaflets and contrasting bright red burrs. All are Z6.

Use Ground cover – suitable for covering large areas in full sun. Can be intermingled with other vigorous ground covers such as *Ajuga* and *Cotula* species for interesting tapestry-type effects.

Acanthus spinosus

Acanthus

ACANTHACEAE

Size and growth form Medium or large clump-forming herbaceous perennials.

Persistence ❉ ❉

Vigorous plants of Mediterranean or west Asian origin, with deeply toothed leaves, and impressive spikes of rather heavily built flowers in midsummer, which turn to statuesque seedheads. All have a tendency to be summer- or at least drought-dormant, making them useful for dry climates with moderate winters – winter or spring growth is lush, and drought avoided simply by dying back. Persistent, though, in moister and cooler climates.

Species and varieties *A. mollis* is the best-known, a large and vigorous plant, handsome but certainly not elegant. *A. spinosus* is also on the big side but has somewhat more refinement, having more deeply toothed leaves. There are various other smaller species. Seedheads of all are roughly similar. Both are Z6.

Use Good for dry shade in warm-summer climates, best in sun or light shade elsewhere. Can be combined with other robust perennials of similar habitats: geraniums, persicarias and so on. Adds a kind of aesthetic weight to groupings of more delicate-looking plants. Can grow to form large stands where a long growing season permits.

Aconitum x *cammarum*

Aconitum Monkshood

RANUNCULACEAE

previous pages *Achillea filipendulina* 'Gold Plate' above *Achillea* 'Gold Plate' in front of *Panicum virgatum*

Achillea Yarrow

ASTERACEAE

Size and growth form Medium-sized clump-forming herbaceous perennials.

Persistence ✸ ✸
Popular border plants of Eurasian origin grown for their finely divided foliage and flat umbel heads of flower, borne in midsummer and available in a variety of colours. Seedheads have an interesting shape, but come in only muddily grey-brown tones. The foliage tends to be persistent through the winter in milder climates.

Species and varieties *A. millefolium* (Z2) is extremely common as a wildflower both in Europe and (as an introduction) in North America. It makes up in environmental tolerance for what it lacks in flower impact – dirty white is the best description, although named forms such as 'Cerise Queen' offer

more interest. *A. filipendulina* (Z3) is a larger plant, to 1.2m tall, with grey-green leaves, its cultivar 'Gold Plate' having flower-/seedheads a magnificent 15cm across. It does well on dry sites. There are numerous hybrids between these two – the colours of the fading flowers of varieties such as 'Fanal', 'Walther Funcke' and 'Wesersandstein' being particularly good value. However, they are reliable over the winter only on very well-drained soils, rotting off in winter damp, and often succeeding better in continental climates. Frequent re-propagation by division is also necessary.
Use The flat flower- and seedhead makes a good contrast with many other shapes – spikes and spires especially. Full sun and good drainage are essential.

Size and growth form Large upright-growing clump-forming perennials.

Persistence ✸ ✸
Robust plants of woodland edge and tall-herb floras across Eurasia, the spikes of hooded flowers, most usually blue, are very distinctive. Flowering times vary between early and late summer. The tall spikes of their seedheads tend to stand out in a habitat where much else is lower or less impressive in the autumn. Monkshoods need fertile, moist soil and protection from strong winds. Most tolerate some shade, and indeed require it in warm-summer climates. All tend to early dormancy in times of drought.

Species and varieties There is a wide range of species and a few hybrids, all very much of a muchness in seedhead terms. Blue-flowered *A. aculeatum* is a particularly tall and strong-growing one, sometimes topping two metres. Most are Z4–6.
Use Aconitums provide structural interest to the plantings of lower-growing and more formless plants, such as geraniums, which tend to thrive in light shade.

Actaea alba

Agapanthus

Actaea

RANUNCULACEAE

Size and growth form Small to medium-sized clump-forming herbaceous perennials.

Persistence ❋❋

Unusual among herbaceous plants in having berries rather than dry seedheads, as such adding an element of autumnal surprise to the shadier areas of the garden. The berries are borne on short spikes and have a distinct calyx at the end. The various species are found across North America and Eurasia. The berries are toxic to humans. Cool or shaded situation required, with humus-rich soil.

Species and varieties *A. rubra* (Z3) has red berries; *A. alba* (Z3) has white (making it the most unusual and visually striking of the genus); *A. spicata* (Z5) has black berries, and *A. erythrocarpa* (Z2) maroon.

Use Best combined with other lovers of cool woodland spots, such as arisaemas, trilliums and tricyrtis.

Former *Cimicifuga* species The inclusion of the genus that used to be known as *Cimicifuga* into *Actaea* is one of those botanical decisions which drives gardeners crazy. For our purposes it is especially annoying, as what distinguishes the two is that the former are tall and have dry seedheads, while the latter are short and have fleshy berries.

Size and growth form Large to very large upright-growing herbaceous perennials.

Persistence ❋❋ / ❋❋❋

Found in woodland-edge habitats across the cool temperate zone, cimicifugas have densely packed and often dramatically tall spikes of white or cream flowers in late summer, which turn into similarly impressive heads of neat little capsules. Their narrowness is elegant, while the fact that they frequently do not grow straight but bend around adventurously adds to their charm. Most are Z3.

Use Cimicifugas add real stature to woodland-edge and other lightly shaded habitats, and provide interest to these environments long after their main season.

Agapanthus African lily

LILIACEAE

Size and growth form Clump-forming herbaceous perennials. Foliage generally around 30cm high, flower- and seedheads to 60cm–1.2m. Potentially spreading.

Persistence ❋❋

Among the most familiar plants of Mediterranean and subtropical gardens, the blue-flowered agapanthus (originally South African) include many which will thrive in sheltered locations in cool temperate climates, flowering in early to midsummer. The strap-shaped leaves of some are evergreen, others not. The seedheads of all are attractive, stout capsules hanging from the rounded umbels – a robust winter statement, especially when massed.

Use The evergreen species are useful for ground cover in shade in warmer climates. Elsewhere the hardier sorts make good border plants, the stout clumps of seedheads a distinct feature for a front-of-border location. In cooler climes they are commonly grown in large tubs on sheltered terraces. Z7–9.

Agastache rugosa 'Liquorice White'

Agastache

LAMIACEAE

Size and growth form The species discussed
are medium-sized short-lived herbaceous
perennials.

Persistence ✹ ✹ ✹
Strongly aromatic (usually minty or medicinal),
agastaches grow fast and furiously, usually
dying out after a few years, unless they happen
to self-sow – which they often do. Far-eastern
A. foeniculum and *A. rugosa* (supposedly Z8)
have short, tight spikes of mauve flowers over
several months from midsummer to autumn,
turning to form tight, well-defined seedheads.
Use Flowering in its first year from seed,
A. foeniculum and hybrids derived from it are
sometimes used in temporary summer
plantings, where the seedheads continue to
provide interest long after many other species
have dissolved into a mush.

Agrostis

POACEAE

Size and growth form The species discussed
is a medium-sized annual grass.

Persistence ✹ ✹
A. nebulosa is just that, nebulous, with
immensely fine flower- and seedheads in
summer and early autumn, looking just like
smoke. The nearest thing to dry ice for the
garden (and longer lasting). May self-sow on
light soils. Native to Spain.

Use Good for combining with other annuals,
or light enough for combining with small dry-
habitat plants like creeping thymes, sedums,
acaenas etc.

Alcea Hollyhock

MALVACEAE

Size and growth form Large to very large
upright-growing, short-lived herbaceous
perennials.

Persistence ✹ ✹
These classic cottage-garden annuals have
flowers in a variety of colours (pretty much
everything that does not involve a blue
pigment, including some near-black) on tall
stems, followed by characteristic mallow-family
seedheads – button-like structures containing
a number of chunky seeds that look vaguely
like miniature pies; indeed, I seem to
remember them featuring as such in children's
games. The garden hybrids are descended
from *A. rosea*, originally from Turkey.
Hollyhocks are short-lived at the best of times,
and are often treated as biennials. Seed sown
one year will produce plants to flower the
next. Once established they will frequently
seed themselves around, being especially
adept at inserting themselves into gaps in
paving and at the base of walls.
Use Combining well with other tall perennials
and biennials, the large flowers and traditional
associations of hollyhocks render them more
suitable for the ornamental garden rather than
the naturalistic. Combine with lupins,
delphiniums and verbascums for the 'olde
Englishe' look.

Allium Ornamental onion

ALLIACEAE/LILIACEAE

Size and growth form Species discussed are
medium-sized to large bulbs.

Persistence ✹ ✹
A group of increasingly popular and often
spectacular bulbs for late spring and early
summer flowering. The so-called 'drumstick'
alliums are semi-desert species from west Asia
which have globe-shaped heads of mauve
flowers atop narrow stems. All require warm
and sunny sites if they are to flower reliably
every year. The leaves are relatively low and
must not be crowded by other plants, at least
until they die down in midsummer.

Allium sphaerocephalum

A. *hollandicum* (often known incorrectly as A. *aflatunense*) has 10cm spherical umbels on metre-high stems with mauve-pink flowers. A. *rosenbachianum* is similar with purple-mauve flowers; A. *stipitatum* has lilac flowers. A. *giganteum* has lilac-pink flowers in 10cm spherical umbels on stems 1.5–2m high. A. *cristophii* has large, slightly flattened heads 20cm across with somewhat metallic-looking pink-purple flowers on stems 30–60cm high. Of similar height, A. *schubertii* is particularly spectacular, with spherical umbels some 30cm across of pale purple flowers (or seed capsules) on stalks of varying lengths, creating a fireworks effect; when dried, it is particularly beloved of flower-arrangers. A. 'Globemaster' is one of a new and growing group of hybrids derived from these species; it has particularly spectacular and wide flowerheads – more like it can be expected to appear in the future.

Most are Z4.

Finally, we must not forget the humble leek (A. *porrum*), which if allowed to flower and seed makes a very good, and cheap, alternative to the above, with a mauve flower the size of a tennis ball on a 1.5m stem, followed by similar size seedheads.

Use As with any bulbs, it is the ease with which alliums can simply be inserted into existing plantings which makes them seductively attractive plants to use. For maximum visual effect they are best grown in loose groups where their style is not cramped by surrounding plants. Their seedheads mature by midsummer and are therefore a feature from this time on, which makes it very important that they are surrounded by plants a good deal lower than themselves for maximum impact. They look particularly effective when spray-painted or dried.

Alstroemeria Peruvian lily

ALSTROEMERIACEAE

Size and growth form Medium to large clump-forming perennials.

Persistence ✿✿

Colourful and often interestingly patterned flowers atop upright stems with linear leaves. Many of the modern hybrids are bred to be sterile (so that they may not be readily propagated, which would negate the investment of the breeders), and so will not produce seedheads, but the species (mostly of Chilean origin), and the old cottage garden *ligtu* hybrids produce intriguing-looking round seedheads, around 1.5cm across. Z8.

Use Vigorous plants for large borders.

Amaranthus

AMARANTHACEAE

Size and growth form Large, upright-growing half-hardy annuals.

Persistence ✿✿

These are among the most interesting and up-and-coming of annuals, with tightly packed elongated flower- and seedheads, in some varieties upright, in others pendent. In most cases the heads are branched. Flower colours vary enormously, and leaves are often tinted, too. The seed is edible, being an excellent source of protein, and the leaves are eaten as a vegetable in many old and new world tropical cultures – being a particular favourite in the Caribbean, where it is known as 'callalloo' in English-based patois. In many species and seed strains the leaves are either tinted or marked with purple, brown or red. Most are Central or South American by origin, and have played an important part in many pre-Columbian cultures.

In cool summer climates, amaranths are best started from seed at a temperature of around 20°C, and planted out after the last frosts. Full sun and fertile soil give best results. Self-sowing may sometimes occur.

Species and varieties A. *caudatus* is the well-known 'love lies bleeding' whose name speaks the melodramatic 'language of flowers' so central to romance in the Victorian era. Its deep cerise-crimson pendent flower- and seedheads can be as long as 60cm.

A. 'Bolivia' has narrow red heads.

A. cruentus has red-shot green pendent flower-/seedheads. Seed strains 'Amont' and 'Golden Giant' have golden-yellow heads on 1.2–2m high plants. 'Chihuahuan' has dark red heads. For those interested in grain production, these plants can produce 500g of seed each.

A. gangeticus 'Tête d'Éléphant' has red-tinged leaves and rich dark red seedheads with a strange trunk-like shape.

A. hypochondriacus has upright heads, maroon or reddish. 'Pygmy Torch' is a useful small-growing seed strain, to around 50cm. 'Intense Purple' grows up to 2.5m with deep red-purple heads and foliage.

A. 'Mercado' is a traditional Mexican variety for grain production, with golden rather than the usual black seeds. The heads are pink-tinged green.

A. 'Plenitude' is an early-maturing variety bred for grain production by the Rodale Research Centre in Pennsylvania. It grows to 1.5m and has red-brown heads.

A. 'Queue de Renard Rouge' ('Red Fox') is a variety with a pendent head, hence the French name which means 'red fox tail'. There is a pale variety – 'Queue de Renard Blanc'.

A. tricolor has far less conspicuous heads, but many forms have colourfully marked foliage.

Use Amaranths combine well with medium-sized and larger annuals for informal summer plantings, needing the full sun and high fertility that such combinations nearly always require. They can also be used in the more ornamental vegetable garden.

Amsonia

APOCYNACEAE

Size and growth form Medium-sized herbaceous perennials.

Persistence ✤✤
The various species in cultivation all seem to have cold, almost pure blue flowers, in early summer, followed by long and narrow pods

(7 x 0.5cm) gathered at the top of the stems, and pointing, somewhat chaotically, in all directions. Yellow autumn foliage. Native to cool temperate zones in both Eurasia and North America, they tend to thrive on drier alkaline soils. Hardiness varies according to species, Z3–7.

Use Front of border plants, or to be combined with other drought-tolerant species in steppe and other wild-style plantings.

Anaphalis

ASTERACEAE

Size and growth form Species discussed are medium-sized clump-forming herbaceous perennials.

Persistence ✤✤
Anaphalis are among the few truly hardy members of the daisy family with the characteristic 'everlasting' type flowerheads typical of some warm-climate family members – where the central zone of the flower and

resultant seedhead is surrounded by papery and persistent bracts. These are white in the case of anaphalis, and are complemented by the grey tone of the foliage. Their midsummer flowering season and relative drought tolerance make them valuable ornamentals. Species are to be found across Northern Hemisphere cool-temperate zones. Most Z3.

Use *Anaphalis* combine well with other small and medium-sized later-flowering perennials, their white seedheads adding a touch of light as other species around them lose their characteristic colours.

Anemone

RANUNCULACEAE

Size and growth form Species discussed here are all large upright-growing, clump-forming herbaceous perennials.

Persistence ✤
The so-called 'Japanese' anemones (some are from China) – *A.* x *hybrida* and *A. hupehensis*,

Anaphalis

Anemone x hybrida

Angelica archangelica

are valued for their profuse midsummer to autumn flowers and ability to survive, and indeed spread, for many years with little attention. The white or pink flowers are followed by bobbly heads 1.5–2cm wide producing a seed with a fluffy coating, for a while briefly resembling disintegrating balls of cotton wool. Z4.

Use Good for low-maintenance plantings in light shade. Combine well with geraniums in such places, as they retain plenty of character long after the geraniums have passed their best.

Angelica

APIACEAE

Size and growth form Medium to large upright-growing biennials.

Persistence ✿✿

A group of umbellifers to be found across the Northern Hemisphere with chunky rather than graceful good looks – broad divided foliage and very rounded flower-/seedheads. All are biennial and can often be relied upon to self-sow.

Species and varieties Giant *A. archangelica* (Z4), a native of northern Europe, grows to

2 x 1.5m, making it a dramatic addition to the larger border or garden, and is a passable substitute for the magnificent (but now deeply unpopular) giant hogweed *Heracleum mantegazzianum*. It has a self-sowing tendency, but this is rarely aggressively expressed – as it is in the heracleum. East Asian *A. gigas* (80cm high) was briefly one of the most fashionable plants around, a dumpy umbellifer transformed into plant cat-walk material by its deep purple colouring, particularly the purple-maroon of the flowers. As a seedhead plant it is less exciting, and its reluctance to self-sow means that most of us have to re-propagate it continually if we want to keep it in our gardens. Of the various other species which occasionally appear in cultivation, one is worth mentioning for its potential future as an even bigger (and therefore better) giant hogweed substitute – 3m high *A. ursina*, from the Russian far east.

Use Statuesque plants for gardens with a reasonable amount of space.

Aquilegia Columbine

RANUNCULACEAE

Size and growth form Medium-sized upright-growing short-lived herbaceous perennials.

Persistence ✿ ✿

Aquilegias are sometimes known as columbines, and occasionally by the cod-historic name of 'granny's bonnets' – did anyone's granny ever wear a hat like an aquilegia flower? They have some of the earliest of seedheads to be produced, developing rapidly after the flowers die in early summer. Their pointy-tipped capsules are carried on stems tall enough to make them interesting at least until they get swamped by taller and later-developing plants. The genus is found across the Northern Hemisphere in cool temperate climates, and a wide range of species has been used to create the hybrids most frequently grown.

Use The innumerable colours (pinks, creams, blues, violets, yellows, reds) of aquilegias make them popular border plants. All are good at self-sowing, the various hybrids and forms of *A. vulgaris* (Z3) especially so, and robust enough for lightly shaded wild-garden situations.

Aralia

ARALIACEAE

Size and growth form Large suckering shrubs and very large clump-forming herbaceous perennials.

Persistence ✿ ✿

The dense clusters of small dark, almost black, berries of aralias hint to the botanically aware of a close relationship to ivy. These follow on from the large panicles, clouds almost, of creamy-white flowers that are produced in late summer or autumn, a boon to late-season nectar-seeking insects. How long the berries last depends on how fast the birds eat them. Aralias in summer are renowned for their foliage, often doubly or even triply pinnate. *Aralia* species can be found in woodland across the cool temperate zone of the Northern Hemisphere.

Aquilegia

Aralia californica

Species and varieties Aralias are divided between those which form woody stems, as high as 4m, suckering to form extensive stands – e.g. *A. elata* (Z4), *A. spinosa* (Z5) – and herbaceous ones, which form large clumps – e.g. *A. cachemirica* (Z7), *A. californica* (Z8), *A. cordata* (Z8). These latter species can, with time, form plants 2.5m high and across.

Use The foliage of aralias lends itself to exotic or heavily architectural planting schemes. Since these plantings frequently offer so little to wildlife, the addition of some aralias helps local biodiversity.

Argemone Prickly poppy

PAPAVERACEAE

Size and growth form Medium-sized to large annuals.

Persistence ✳ ✳

Easy, vigorous annuals with deeply indented grey foliage often vaguely resembling an oak leaf in shape, and yellow or white poppy-like flowers. Inflated pods some 3–4cm long, with distinct spines, open at the apex to release the seed, the whole resembling some sort of urchin-like sea creature. Most Z8.

Use Effective in naturalistic annual plantings; generally too loose for anything more formal.

Arum

ARACEAE

Size and growth form Small to medium clump-forming herbaceous perennials.

Persistence ✳ ✳

Another one of those oddities among herbaceous perennials with berries; they all seem to be woodland plants for some reason. Arums have the classic flowers of the family – mysterious hooded leaf-like spathes and a central rod-shaped spadix – followed by berries clustered tightly around the stem, which is nearly always orange-red. The plants are native to forest habitats in Europe and the Mediterranean region.

Use Arums need cool, shaded or lightly shaded habitats, and once established naturalize readily. *Arum italicum* 'Pictum',

81

Asclepias incarnata

A.i. 'Marmoratum' (Z6) and other varieties of the species are grown for their ornamental white-marked foliage.

Asclepias

APOCYNACEAE

Size and growth form Large clump-forming herbaceous perennials.

Persistence ❋

Asclepias have distinct pointed seedpods packed with large seeds with silky white hairs to carry them away on the wind. The flowers vary considerably between the species, as does the foliage. All are North American in origin.

Species and varieties Butterfly weed, *A. tuberosa* (Z3), is well known as a prairie plant and often included in wildflower plantings. *A. incarnata* (Z3) and *A. speciosa* (Z2) both have large foliage and grow to around 1.5–2m.

Use Some species are used as a part of native planting schemes. Those with large and exotic-looking foliage make good border plants.

Asphodeline

ASPHODELACEAE

Size and growth form Medium-sized herbaceous perennial.

Persistence ❋ ❋

A. lutea (Z7) has spikes of golden-yellow flowers in early summer on intriguingly twisted stems; they are followed by almost perfectly spherical seedheads which open and scatter their seed by early autumn, disintegrating soon after. A plant of dry landscapes from south-eastern Europe, which *en masse* is quite spectacular in flower. The seedheads are a strong visual feature in summer drought conditions.

Use Best grown with smaller, spreading varieties of *Origanum*, *Clinopodium*, *Calamintha* and *Thymus* to make the most of its stature. Good on hot, barren sites.

Aster divaricatus

Aster

ASTERACEAE

Size and growth form Medium to very large upright-growing clump-forming herbaceous perennials.

Persistence ❋

Asters are popular for their profuse late-season flowering. This is followed by equally profuse seeding, but from heads which rarely make much of an impression. They are widely distributed across the cool temperate zones of the Northern Hemisphere, with the most decorative species coming from eastern North America.

Species and varieties Most impact is provided by white-flowered *A. umbellatus* (Z3), which has white seedheads on 2m stems that can really shine for a month or so in the autumn. White-flowered woodland-edge *A. divaricatus* (60cm) and the mauve-flowered variety 'Twilight' (50 x 40cm) have seedheads with a bit more character than most (both Z4). Violet/purple flowered *A. amellus* (Z5) (50–70cm) has quite large heads packed with fawn seed. *A. ericoides* (Z3) (80–100cm) has tiny pale heads, only a few weeks after the last of the blue, pink or cream flowers have finished, making it look as if the dark dead foliage has been splattered with paint.

Use For borders and wild gardens, in conjunction with other late-flowering plants like eupatoriums, helianthus, rudbeckias etc.

Astilbe

ROSACEAE

Size and growth form Most are medium to large clump-forming herbaceous perennials.

Persistence ❋❋

Hailing originally from moist environments in Eurasia, astilbes are grown for the showy flowerheads, in reds, pinks and white, composed of thousands of tiny flowers packed into upright panicles. Their flowers in early summer tend to have an air of being stiff and unrelaxed, but in the autumn, as everything around them in the damper parts of the garden where they thrive begins to collapse

Astilbe x *arendsii* 'Else Schluck'

into the particular state of untidiness that moisture-loving plants have at this time, this stiffness comes into its own, their brown seedheads a beacon of relative order. All are vigorous plants for moist soils and waterside locations.

Species and varieties Hybrids and cultivars vary considerably in how wide and loose the flower-/seedheads are – the x *arendsii* hybrids (Z4) tend to be open and plume-like. *A. chinensis* (Z3) varieties are tighter and more upright, giving them more winter impact: *A.c.* var. *davidii* (1.6m) is a good larger form, 'Visions' a small one (40cm high), while *A.c.* var. *pumila* grows to only 25cm.

Use Astilbes look best in clumps or groups among other waterside and wetland plants. Given enough space, they are spectacular *en masse*.

Astrantia Masterwort

APIACEAE

Size and growth form Medium-sized herbaceous perennials.

Persistence ❋

Astrantias are European woodland plants with a uniquely shaped flowerhead composed of small flowers in a button-shaped umbel surrounded by a ruff of pointed bracts. They flower for months on end from early to late summer, with moderately interesting seedheads whose main feature is the now-brown ruff. Z4.

Use Ideal for cool lightly shaded locations and, given their propensity for self-sowing, for wild-garden areas.

Atriplex

CHENOPODIACEAE

Size and growth form The species discussed is a large, upright-growing annual.

Persistence ❋ ❋

A. hortensis var. *rubra* (Z6) is a plant of Asian origin grown for its dark red foliage. It was once cultivated as a vegetable for the spinach-like leaves. It has relatively inconspicuous flowers but large seeds, which hang profusely from the upright stems. Often vigorously self-sowing.

Use Effective when mixed with other annuals in informal summer plantings or allowed to self-sow spontaneously through borders.

Bouteloua Gramma

POACEAE

Size and growth form Medium-sized perennial grass.

Persistence ❋ ❋

Distinct and attractive one-sided flowers and seedheads above dense tussocks of foliage. Both species discussed are very tough plants, originating as they do from the dry short-grass prairie region of North America. They are heat- and drought-tolerant and take a certain amount of foot-traffic. In northern and maritime climates, a warm situation is vital.

Species and varieties *B. curtipendula*, side-

Atriplex hortensis var. *rubra*

oats gramma (Z4), has oat-like spikelets which all fall to one side of the stem, while *B. gracilis*, blue gramma (Z3), has small comb-like spikelets, thought by some to resemble mosquito larvae – hence another common name, mosquito grass.

Use As a consituent of short-grass prairie or steppe planting schemes or in borders alongside shorter drought-tolerant and later-flowering perennials such as species of *Coreopsis* or *Origanum*. A companion for *Pennisetum* or smaller *Stipa* species.

Briza Quaking grass

POACEAE

Size and growth form Small to medium-sized annual and perennial herbaceous grasses.

Persistence ❋

The quaking grasses have a very distinct shape, difficult to describe beyond saying they are like the jointed bodies of an insect or marine arthropod. Americans think they look like rattlesnake tails, hence one of their

common names – rattlesnake grass. They owe the name quaking grass to the habit of the flower and seedheads moving in the slightest breeze. Of European and Mediterranean region origin.

Species and varieties *B. media* (Z4) has small heads (6 x 4mm) and is perennial. *B. maxima* has large heads (15 x 10mm) and is annual, but once introduced to a garden it can self-sow to problem dimensions. The latter is particularly effective dried in winter flower arrangements.

Use *B. media* consorts well with other smaller grasses such as *Melica* species, and with lower-growing flowering perennials. *B. maxima* makes a good companion for robust cottage-garden annuals like *Nigella* and *Calendula*.

Calamagrostis

POACEAE

Size and growth form Large clump-forming herbaceous perennial grasses.

Persistence ❄ ❄ ❄

This is a genus of strong-growing and generally upright grasses from Eurasia, of which two have become extremely popular as garden plants. *C. x acutiflora* 'Stricta' and *C. x acutiflora* 'Karl Foerster' (Z5) are so similar as to be almost identical, both growing to around 1.6 to 2m and producing stiffly upright flowerheads in early summer, the straw-coloured stems then standing until … the gardener decides to cut them down, generally in late winter. Their strength is remarkable, and is illustrated by their popularity in gardens along the US East Coast, where James van Sweden notes that 'they bend over in a hurricane and bounce back up'.

Full sun is essential, as otherwise the stems become weak at the nodes, which can then break.

Use The long season of these plants makes them invaluable as continuity elements in the garden, so linking the seasons. Their upright habit contrasts well with the more rounded forms of other plants and also suggests their use as a repeating element to establish rhythm and echo, so linking spaces.

Calamagrostis

Campanula

CAMPANULACEAE

Size and growth form Species discussed are medium to large herbaceous perennials and biennials.

Persistence 🌣

A varied group of nearly always blue- or violet/mauve-flowered plants from Europe and western Asia. The small capsule-type seedheads do not last long, but have an intricate beauty even as they decay. Among the best are those woodland-edge species which are tall enough to thrust their seed capsules into our field of vision.

Species and varieties *C. latifolia* (Z3) and *C. trachelium* (Z3) are two well-known species at around 80cm–1.2m x 30cm. *C. lactiflora* (Z5) is larger at 2m x 80cm. *C. pyramidalis* (Z8) is a less hardy plant, a biennial which forms a dramatically tall spire of purple-blue flowers.

Use All of these can be grown in both the border and wilder-style plantings.

Cardiocrinum

LILIACEAE

Size and growth form Very large bulbous perennials.

Persistence 🌣🌣/🌣🌣🌣

A lily on steroids, *C. giganteum* (Z7) can grow to 3–4.5m tall, with massive creamy-white flowers in early summer. The seedheads are also impressively voluptuous, 6cm long and held upright on muscular stems. Plants are effectively monocarpic, leaving small bulbs which take several years to build up to flowering size again. Light shade and humus-rich, moisture-retentive soil are vital.

Use One of the finest of garden plants when grown in groups in woodland.

Carlina

ASTERACEAE

Size and growth form Species discussed are low to medium short-lived herbaceous perennials.

Persistence 🌣🌣🌣

Campanula

C. acaulis (Z4) is a thistle with spectacularly large flowerheads (up to 15cm across) with silvery-white rays. In its native European Alps it hugs the ground, but in lowland gardens it is more likely to reach 40cm. Along with gentians and edelweiss, it is something of an alpine symbol, appearing on endless souvenirs and postcards.
Use Rockeries, gravel gardens or other well-drained situations.

Catalpa Indian bean tree

BIGNONIACEAE

Size and growth form Large deciduous trees.
Persistence ✻✻✻
White flowers in large panicles in early summer are followed by masses of narrow 40cm long dark pods, which can adorn the branches for much of the winter. Along with large heart-shaped leaves, they make this tree ornamental for a long season. North American *C. bignonioides* (Z5) is the best known.
Use Catalpas can be kept pruned or pollarded, making them ideal for urban gardens or as street trees.

Centaurea

ASTERACEAE

Size and growth form Large upright-growing clump-forming herbaceous perennials and some annuals.

Centaurea nervosa

Cephalaria alpina

Persistence ✻
A large Eurasian genus with distinctive composite flowerheads whose base (the involucre) is clothed in bracts, technically involucral bracts, the shape of which is an important characteristic for identification. In some species these are very attractive when seen close to, both when the plants are in bud and for a short while after flowering.
Species and varieties *C. nervosa* (Z4) and several related species have particularly fine bracts and mauvy-pink flowers on 60–80cm high stems. *C. solstitialis* is an annual (50cm) with yellow flowers and bracts formed into long and persistent spines.
Use Many centaureas would be valuable border plants for midsummer flowering if it were not for their annoying habit of flopping over. Grown as wildflower-meadow plants on poor soils, and in competition with other plants, they are less likely to do this. The dark seedheads are a valuable point of interest in end-of-season wildflower meadows.

Cephalaria

DIPSACACEAE

Size and growth form Very large upright-growing clump-forming herbaceous perennials.

Persistence ✻✻
The only commonly grown species, Caucasian *C. gigantea* (Z3), is valued for its exquisitely pale yellow flowers in midsummer, followed by large button-like seedheads. *C. alpina* is similar.
Use A bulky plant for large borders or lush wild-garden plantings. The seedheads are best appreciated in silhouette against the sky.

Cercis Judas tree, redbud

FABACEAE

Size and growth form Small deciduous trees.
Persistence ✻✻
All have relatively large seedpods hanging in generous quantities from twigs and branches throughout the autumn. When just mature they are a distinct red-brown in colour and are quite spectacular when lit up by low sunlight. The late spring flowers are bright pink, and are profuse and showy.
Species and varieties The Judas tree, *C. siliquastrum* (Z6), is a native of the Mediterranean region, with flowers and seedheads borne on both branches and twigs. Other species such as the North American *C. canadensis* (Z4) are similar, but bear flowers only on the twigs.

Cercis siliquastrum

Use Commonly grown as ornamental trees, their small size makes them appropriate for smaller gardens. They have some tolerance of light shade and are thus useful for open woodland.

Chasmanthium

POACEAE

Size and growth form Medium-sized herbaceous perennial grass.

Persistence ✷✷✷

Somewhat like an iron-flattened quaking grass or oat, the seedheads of *C. latifolium* (*Uniola latifolia*) (Z5) hang from upright stems. Tolerant of light shade. A tough and easy plant from woodland-edge habitats in eastern North America.

Use A distinctive appearance and the tolerance, rare in grasses, for shade make this a useful plant for winter interest among lower-growing flowering perennials.

Chelone Turtlehead

SCROPHULARIACEAE

Size and growth form Medium-sized clump-forming herbaceous perennial, spreading strongly.

Persistence ✷✷

The North American perennial *C. glabra* (Z3) has squat pink flowers in dense heads in late summer. These are followed by similarly solid-

Chasmanthium latifolium

Chelone glabra

looking seedheads with open mouths, hence the popular name. (Indeed, the turtle referred to is probably the infamous snapper turtle, which will never let go of whatever it sinks its formidable jaws into.) It prefers moister soils or a little shade.

Use In extensive border or wild-garden plantings, where its strongly spreading habit can make a valuable contribution.

Clarkia

ONAGRACEAE

Size and growth form Small to medium-sized annuals.

Persistence ✳ ✳

A North American genus, with bright flowers usually in reds, pinks and purples, and masses of small narrow seedheads which split open almost as far as the base to reveal straw-coloured interior surfaces.

Use Clarkias have long been used in loose cottage-garden-style summer plantings. The light seedheads help to brighten up such plant combinations if their remains are left over winter.

Clematis

RANUNCULACEAE

Size and growth form Herbaceous plants and climbers with woody persistent stems.

Persistence ✳ ✳ ✳

Many clematis species produce plentiful spherical seedheads, formed from the massed fluffy tips of the achenes (the structure that encloses each seed). In the right conditions – low autumn or winter sunlight – these can be a spectacular pearly-silver adornment to the landscape from the hedgerows of England to the deserts of Pakistan, and the hills of New Zealand, too, for this is a very widespread genus.

Species and varieties Of the vast number in cultivation, only some of the species, and almost none of the familiar large-flowered hybrids, can be relied upon for a good display of seedheads. The yellow-flowered *C. orientalis* (Z6) and *C. tangutica* (Z4) can be spectacular in seed, when their 15m stems are draped over a large tree or wall. *C. vitalba* (Z4), the 'old man's beard' of European woodland-edge and scrubland habitats, is a glorious sight when lit by winter sunlight – silver jewellery poured over trees – but it is so large (to 20m) and rampant and its flowers so insignificant that few would have it in any but the largest and wildest of gardens.

All the small-growing atragene section, such as *C. alpina* (Z3) and *C. macropetala* (Z3), have good seedheads, but because they flower in late spring, the seedheads mature in summer and are liable to be overlooked. Most grow to around 2–3m high.

C. fusca (Z5) is also good. Of the scandent and herbaceous species, *C. integrifolia* (Z3) is the most striking.

Use Many of those that bear good seedheads are vigorous climbers needing stout supports. They are perhaps best appreciated when allowed to scramble up large trees, where the seedheads can catch winter's sparse sunbeams. The smaller atragene section species are good for use on fences, or in mixed border situations, clambering over shrubs or up dedicated structures such as obelisks.

Clematis 'Helios'

Clinopodium

LAMIACEAE

Size and growth form Small clump-forming
herbaceous perennials.

Persistence ❋❋❋

Neat and tight little whorls of rose-pink
flowers stiffen into very long-lasting seedheads
which create a good winter impression.
A plant of dry-meadow and steppe habitats
in Europe and west Asia.

Use Effective in dry-meadow plantings and
with other small-growing drought-tolerant
species. Combines well with the small grasses
of such habitats, such as *Festuca*, *Sesleria* etc.

Colutea

FABACEAE

Size and growth form Small to medium-sized
shrubs.

Persistence ❋❋❋

The English name of *C. arborescens* (Z5) says
it all – bladder senna. The pods, generally
around 5–8cm long, are inflated, and make
a noise when squeezed to bursting point.
They can also be decorative, and are certainly
a curiosity. Most species have attractively fine
pinnate foliage and flowers in orange or
yellow shades. The species in cultivation are
of Eurasian origin.

Use Tolerant of a wide range of conditions,
coluteas are particularly useful as shrubs to
combine with herbaceous perennials in mixed
borders, as their root systems are relatively
uncompetitive. They also fix nitrogen at the
roots and so do not deplete soil of nutrients,
which is another factor rendering them good
neighbours.

Cortaderia Pampas grass

POACEAE

Size and growth form Large to very large
evergreen perennial grasses.

Persistence ❋❋❋

Few plants evoke criticism and disdain like
pampas grass. A native of Argentina, gardeners
are commonly heard to say it is best left there.

Cotinus coggygria

A shame, as in the right place it is a truly magnificent plant, the fluffy white plumes standing proud of the arching clumps of dark green leaves. Its downfall has been in the hands of people who, in the damning (and snobbish) words of a colleague, 'seem to think that it enhances their social status by having it on their front lawn' – overuse in small gardens by people on the wrong side of the tracks, in other words.

Species and varieties *C. selloana* (Z8) is the species normally seen, with a variety of cultivars, some having variegated foliage such as the gold-edged 'Aureolineata', some dwarf such as the 1–1.2m 'Pumila', some even larger than average, like the 3.5m 'Sunningdale Silver', or with a colour to the plumes, like pink-flushed 'Rosea'.

C. *richardii* is a quieter plant from New Zealand with golden-brown plumes to 1.2–3m.

Use Magnificent as a specimen in a very large lawn, but undeniably a cliché. Perhaps most effective when grown among shrubs with winter interest such as coloured-stemmed willows or dogwoods.

Cotinus Smoke bush

ANACARDIACEAE

Size and growth form Medium-sized deciduous shrubs.

Persistence ❋ ❋
Attractive rounded leaves and dramatic seedheads make *C. coggygria* (Z5) a popular shrub. The seedheads form a fawn-coloured filamentous mass, about 20cm wide, looking from a distance like puffs of smoke. Good yellowy or orangy autumn colour, too.

Species and varieties Eurasian *C. coggygria* 'Royal Purple' has purple-flushed foliage, and pinky seedheads; 'Notcutt's Variety' red foliage and pink-purple seedheads. North American *C. obovatus* has larger (to 30cm) seedheads.

Use Effective in large gardens or parks in mixed or shrub borders. Alternatively it can be kept coppiced, when it is more likely to sucker, and then be combined with vigorous perennials.

Crocosmia Montbretia

IRIDACEAE

Size and growth form Medium-sized herbaceous perennials.

Persistence ✻✻

A number of species from the southern temperate regions of South America have given rise to a great many hybrids, all in shades of orange and yellow, ideal for mild and moist maritime climates. Flowers are followed by seedheads which are rather insignificant, but arranged on rather stiffly elegant stems. Z7.

Use The seedheads are best seen in silhouette or uncrowded by other plants.

Cynara Globe artichoke/cardoon

ASTERACEAE

Size and growth form The species discussed is a very large clump-forming herbaceous perennial.

Persistence ✻✻

C. cardunculus (Z6) has large flowerheads (up to 15cm) with purple florets and somewhat spiny involucral bracts (as in *Centaurea*) which dry to form dramatic seedheads. Originally Mediterranean, but now widely cultivated as a vegetable. The early year growth of the vast silvery and deeply toothed leaves is as fine a spectacle of foliage as can be found in the border at this time.

Use Can be a feature of the decorative vegetable garden or a bulky talking-point in the larger border.

Datisca

DATISCACEAE

Size and growth form Large herbaceous perennial.

Persistence ✻✻

Datisca cannabina (Z6) has lush and delicate foliage, resembling cannabis only to the most intoxicated, or to ill-trained and suspicious members of the police. The flowers are greeny yellow and relatively insignificant, but on female plants are followed by what can only be described as bead curtains of 1cm-wide seedheads on stems which cascade down from a central stem. Both sexes will be needed for successful seedhead production.

Use An unusual plant for borders. It looks good alongside seasonal exotica such as cannas, dahlias or *Ricinus communis*.

Crocosmia 'Lucifer'

Cynara cardunculus

Daucus carota

Daucus Wild carrot

APIACEAE

Size and growth form The species discussed is a medium-sized biennial.

Persistence ✿ ✿

Wild, or indeed cultivated, carrots form a distinctive seedhead whereby the usual umbel shape of the Apiaceae family bends inward, even before the rather grubby white summer-borne flowers are over. Originally Eurasian, it is now well established in the North American flora, where its common name is Queen Anne's lace. Particularly good for poorer soils.

Use A component of many wildflower seed mixes, wild carrot frequently dominates the first few years of any resulting meadow, before being displaced by longer-lived species. Conventional garden carrot seed is as good as any for seedheads.

Decaisnea

LARDIZABALACEAE

Size and growth form Large deciduous shrubs.

Persistence ✿ ✿

Creamy-greeny flowers in early summer lead

to pod-shaped fruit with an extraordinary blue-grey colouring. The foliage is pinnate and a feature in its own right. From the lower slopes of the Himalayas in China, they need a warm and sheltered site. In cooler climates their fruiting can be unreliable. Only *D. fargesii* (Z5) is at all common in cultivation.

Use As an exotic feature plant in suitable warm locations.

Deschampsia

POACEAE

Size and growth form Medium-sized, more or less evergreen perennial grass.

Persistence ✿

D. cespitosa (Z4) is a common grass of woodland habitats and poor soils throughout northern Europe, with tiny flower- and seedheads which form an attractive cloudy mass in late summer to mid-autumn. Some tolerance of shade, but little of competition from surrounding plants

Use Seedheads visually present a very 'matt' appearance in the border, a contrast to more defined grassy shapes. Complemented by late bright flower colours: rudbeckias, echinaceas,

Deschampsia cespitosa 'Gold Veil' ('Goldschleier')

shorter asters. Grown *en masse*, it can be spectacular, especially if plants with distinct seedheads like species of *Digitalis* or *Verbascum* are grown in among it.

Digitalis Foxglove

SCROPHULARIACEAE

Size and growth form Large or very large biennials or short-lived perennials.

Persistence ✿ ✿ ✿

Digitalis provide one of the most distinctive genera of woodland-edge habitats in Europe and west Asia, with their often tall spikes of flower, followed by capsules which effectively broadcast large quantities of the fine seed around the parent plant. All flower from early to midsummer.

Species and varieties *D. ferruginea* (Z4) is quite simply one of the best seedhead plants around when grown in large numbers, the small and very hard seed capsules densely clustered on tall stems (up to 1.8m), the whole only around 4cm across. For sheer elegance of line, they are unbeatable; in misty weather particularly they stand out with an air of mystery. The flowers are not particularly colourful but deserve close inspection for their intricate patterns of brown, fawn and cream. A plant of enormous sophistication.

While the above might be art gallery material, *D. purpurea* (Z4) is the cheap print – large and proudly pink flowers on stems 1.5–2m tall, turning to roughly cone-shaped seedheads which split in half but remain firmly attached to the stems, giving it distinct winter value.

Use Easy to naturalize through self-sowing, at least on lighter soils, in full sun or lightly shaded sites. When grown *en masse* they are highly effective in bringing structure to wooded or shaded areas in the garden. The fact that they are narrow plants enables them to be effective in confined spaces.

opposite *Digitalis ferruginea*

Dipsacus

Echinacea pallida

Echinops niveum

Dipsacus Teasel

DIPSACACEAE

Size and growth form Large biennials.

Persistence ✻ ✻ ✻

One of the most robustly weather-defiant of herbaceous plants, the common teasel *D. fullonum* (Z3) is a superb plant for large-scale winter effects, standing proud while all around is a soggy mess. The large thimble-shaped and egg-sized seedheads follow a midsummer display of tiny lilac flowers set among coarse spiny bracts. The seedheads have traditionally been grown for the carding of wool and indeed are sometimes still used for this purpose commercially. Widespread across Eurasia.

Use A vigorously seeding biennial, teasel may well become a problem in some gardens. Best in wild-garden situations, even among rough grass, where occasional ground disturbance may be enough to keep them regenerating for many years. In the wild often found with umbellifers – a practice which could well work in the garden, perhaps alongside other vigorous self-sowing biennials like *Verbascum* and *Oenothera*.

Echinacea

ASTERACEAE

Size and growth form Large upright-growing herbaceous perennials.

Persistence ✻ ✻

One of the most popular genera of North American prairie plants, with many cultivars of *E. purpurea* (Z3) in particular becoming commercially widely available, all of which are excellent and showy long-season plants. The flowers open in midsummer, the last ray florets falling off in mid-autumn to leave big dark cone-shaped seedheads. After a month or so, these release their seed leaving a persistent light-coloured central cone surrounded by a ruff of pointed bracts.

Use In border or wilder prairie-style plantings echinacea heads make fine points of definition.

Echinops Globe thistle

ASTERACEAE

Size and growth form Species in cultivation are large to very large upright, clump-forming herbaceous perennials.

Persistence ✻

Robust European and west Asian perennials

with deeply toothed, rather thistly leaves, and flowers gathered together in almost perfectly spherical balls, which unfortunately disintegrate soon after the seed has ripened. Most Z3.

Use Although they have a short season, echinops heads are wonderful if silhouetted against a paler or fuzzy background. Most are plants for the larger border, or wild garden.

Echium

BORAGINACEAE

Size and growth form Those listed here are large to very large short-lived perennials.

Persistence ✻ ✻ ✻

The massed blue of the Eurasian *E. vulgare* (to 60cm) in many limestone soils or old quarries can be impressive, and the bulky looking spikes of seedheads have some winter interest. *E. russicum* is similar but larger, with dark red flowers, a classic plant of dry-steppe habit. Its multi-branched seedhead can be rather impressive and stands out above low grasses.

Use In dry, thin soils or gravel gardens, where biennials can easily regenerate, these are good

opposite *Echinops ritro* subsp. *ruthenicus*

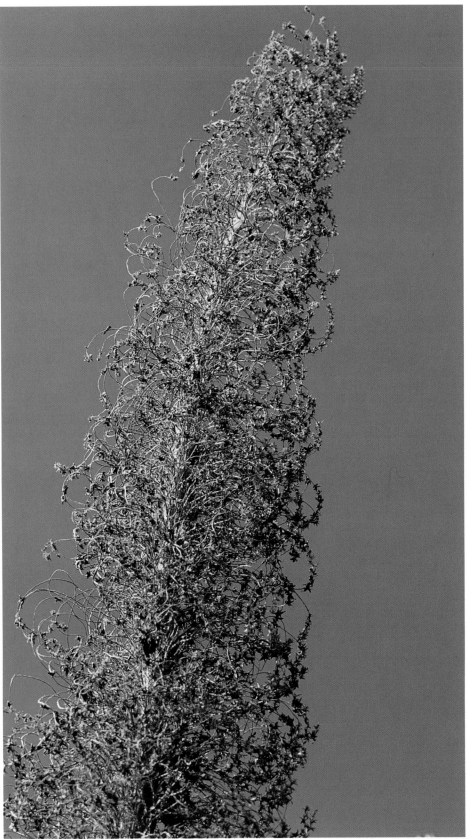

Echium pininana

plants to have alongside verbascums and other short-lived species to add to winter interest.

There are other echiums which, through the peculiar genetic circumstances that seem to prevail among many island floras, have turned into giants. Although the seedheads themselves have little intrinsic interest, when there are several tens of thousands of them packed on to one bendy rocket-shaped head, the result is spectacular. The giant echiums found on some of the mid-Atlantic islands are plants with quite definite 'surreal appeal'. Being monocarpic, dying spectacularly after scattering what must be millions of seed, the following species need to be regularly resown to ensure you have them every year, although in milder gardens this will scarcely be necessary as they are capable of self-sowing with great abandon. Where their hardiness is questionable, the ingenious can protect them from a few degrees of frost with fleece or a miniature greenhouse of plastic as the giant flower spike does not emerge until their final year of life – usually the third.

The Canary Island *E. pininana* is the most commonly seen of the giants, with blue flowers, 3–4m. When these are seen through an early morning mist, the mind inevitably turns to thoughts of extra-terrestrials. *E. simplex* and *E. wildpretii* are similar.

Use Made for the 'exotic' garden, or indeed anywhere where spectacular architectural impact is desired. They do well by the coast, benefiting from the mild climate and seemingly resistant to wind and salt-spray – they have even naturalized along the coast of Britain's Scilly Isles.

Eragrostis Love grass

POACEAE

Size and growth form Small to large herbaceous perennial grasses.

Persistence ❉ ❉
The so-called love grasses are distinctive for the very open, airy nature of their flower- and seedheads. They are widely distributed over the tropics, but a few are hardy enough to grow in cool temperate zone gardens.

Species and varieties African love grass, *E. curvula* (Z7), is the best known, with hair-like foliage and big sprays of fine seedheads of dark olive, fading to grey-brown. The plant is drought-tolerant and in cooler climes it must have good drainage. *E. trichoides* (Z5) has huge seedheads, which start off as silver-pink and then fade to silver-grey. Both of these grow to around 80cm; slightly smaller is *E. spectabilis* (Z5) with purple flowers fading to soft cream seedheads; the foliage can colour reddish in the autumn.

Use These grasses make a misty out-of-focus contrast to more defined shapes in low to medium-height herbaceous plantings. *E. curvula* has a long history as an erosion control on slopes.

Eremurus Foxtail lily
ASPHODELACEAE

Size and growth form Large to very large tuberous-rooted herbaceous perennials.

Persistence ❋ ❋

Tall and elegantly narrow spikes of flowers make these some of the most striking of all early summer flowering plants. There is a range of species and hybrids in cultivation, with flowers in shades of white, cream, fawn and yellow. The seedheads are round and by virtue of the shape and size of the heads can be an emphatic feature. Native to the mountain deserts of eastern Asia, *Eremurus* can be successful and spectacular plants in gardens if they are given the right conditions – very well-drained and fertile soil, and an absence of competition. Z5.

Use Ideal for dry situations, and particularly for steppe-style naturalistic plantings, where their great virtue is that they are so much taller than everything else. Like many other plants with a similar shape, they are best appreciated in loose groups.

Eriogonum Wild buckwheat
POLYGONACEAE

Size and growth form Small to medium herbaceous perennials and subshrubs.

Persistence ❋ ❋/❋ ❋ ❋

Tough, drought-tolerant plants common in the American West. Many have considerable ornamental potential with strawlike flowers in a variety of colours (yellow, pink, white). The bracts which surround the flowers stay on around the seedheads. Eriogonums are among the most useful plants for butterfly larvae.

Use For dry gardens, or rockeries and other well-drained sites. They are best mixed with other low-growing grey-foliage plants or smaller bunch grasses.

Eryngium
APIACEAE

Size and growth form Small to very large clump-forming herbaceous perennials, some biennials.

Persistence ❋ ❋/❋ ❋ ❋

Looking like thistles, but confusingly members of the umbellifer family (Apiaceae), eryngiums provide us with some of the best structure plants for borders and open garden situations. They are unfortunately sometimes dubbed 'sea hollies' by those writers and nurserymen who seem to think that latinate names strike fear into the hearts of the gardening public. Unfortunate in that only one regularly lives by the sea, the European *E. maritimum*, which happens to be the one practically ungrowable plant in the genus, at least in cool temperate gardens – I have, however, heard it highly praised as a plant for Californian gardens!

The deeply toothed leaves of most species are a perfect complement to the thimble-shaped flower-/seedheads and their surrounding thistle-like bracts. Species of European origin flower in early summer, Americans in late summer.

Species and varieties *E. agavifolium* (Z7) is an Argentinian species with spiny-edged strap-like green leaves and large dumpy-looking greeny-white flowerheads which turn to prominent brown seedheads. To 1.5m. Dislikes drying out.

E. alpinum (Z4) has soft outer bracts, a good

Eryngium

Eryngium giganteum

blue when in flower. It also dislikes drying out. From European alpine meadows. 70cm.

E. *bourgatii* (Z5) is only 40cm high, forming a mass of silver and grey-green leaves with blue-green flowerheads surrounded by spine-like bracts. Persistent silvery-brown seedheads. Drier soils. From southern Europe.

E. *giganteum* (Z4) is a biennial from Turkey, with silvery bracts surrounding blue-grey flowerheads which turn into dark brown seedheads. A great self-sower, it is spectacular *en masse* in the early autumn, the bracts being the most prominent element. Known as

Miss Willmott's ghost for the Edwardian lady gardener who secretly scattered seed in gardens she visited, so that her presence would always be there. It unfortunately does not stand wet weather well. 1m.

E. *pandanifolium* (Z8) is a spectacular evergreen species which forms clumps of narrow spiny-edged leaves and sends up 4m spikes in late autumn with small purple flowerheads. From Brazil and Argentina.

E. *proteiflorum* (Z8) is a Mexican species with spiny leaves and extended ivory bracts around a small flowerhead. Dislikes winter damp. 80cm.

E. *yuccifolium* (Z4) is a prairie plant with very rounded heads with prominent bracts, to 1.2m.

E. *variifolium* (Z5) is a North African with brown seedheads surrounded by silvery-grey elongated spiny-looking bracts, contrasting with dark glossy green leaves. The flower-heads are blue. 40cm.

Use Most are good plants for average border conditions, and some flourish on dry stony soils. All, however, look drought-tolerant, even if they are not, and are therefore popular in plantings which seek to create an exotic or desert-like ambiance alongside kniphofias and

Erysimum hybrid

yuccas, or in gravel gardens. Their form is an ideal contrast to the rounded shapes of many Mediterranean-climate subshrubs such as lavenders and the soft linearity of grasses.

Erysimum Wallflower

BRASSICACEAE

Size and growth form Medium-sized short-lived perennials.

Persistence ✸✸

Although the genus *Erysimum* is scattered across the Northern Hemisphere, the common and ever-popular 'wallflower' is derived from *E. cheiri*, commonly seen on old walls or ruins. Spring flowers in warm shades are followed in summer by long thin seedpods which split open along both sides to the base, giving the plants a somewhat spiky (and let us be honest, somewhat untidy) appearance. Z4.

Use A good accompaniment to more rounded seedhead shapes.

Eupatorium

Eupatorium

ASTERACEAE

Size and growth form Species discussed are large to very large upright, clump-forming perennials.

Persistence ✸✸✸

The fluffy, light-coloured seeds of eupatoriums spend only a few weeks on the plant before being blown off to new homes. The stems and old seedhead framework remain, however, and are generally very weather-dependent, hence my high persistence rating. As such they make good winter structure. All tend to flower in mid- or late summer.

Species and varieties *E. cannabinum* (Z5) is a rather undistinguished European plant with

flesh-coloured flowers, but is useful for giving some structural interest to wild plantings on moist soils. Quite shade-tolerant if the soil is moist enough. Any resemblance to *Cannabis sativa* is apparent only to those who have over-indulged in the drug. 1.2m.

E. fistulosum, *E. maculatum* and *E. purpureum* (Z4–5) – Jo-Pye weed – constitute one of those 'species-complexes' which provide material for doctoral research in botany and confusion to the rest of us. All have pale pink flowers and stout stems. Frequenting moister spots in eastern and central North America, the stout stems stand winter well, darkly etched against the snow. 1.6–3.5m tall, forming dense clumps which

Ferula

spread out remarkably little.

Use Plants for the larger border, or prairie-style plantings. All look good arching out over water from riverbanks, or as upright company for the large-leaved genera which are typical of bog-garden settings – *Gunnera*, *Rheum* and *Rodgersia*.

Ferula Giant fennel

APIACEAE

Size and growth form Very large short-lived herbaceous perennial.

Persistence ✾ ✾

The whitened hollow winter stems are supposedly what Prometheus used to hide fire in, so that he could smuggle it to the human race. Great mounds of finely divided dark green foliage and large heads of greeny-yellow are succeeded by the usual umbelliferous seedhead, but on a magnificently tall stem. Biennial or monocarpic in their native Mediterranean and west Asian habitats, they are reported as being soundly perennial in the lusher conditions of cool temperate zone gardens. The foliage is at its most lush in the winter in Mediterranean climate zones, and may be summer-dormant. *Ferula communis* (Z8) is the most commonly grown of several species, all of which produce flowerheads to 4–5m.

Use Magnificent among the ruin-fields of the vanished city of Salamis on the shores of north Cyprus, they can be a bit of an oddity if grown on their own in the plantsman's garden. Best to grow several together, as a border feature, or as part of a deliberately dramatic or exoticist feature.

Fibigia

BRASSICACEAE

Size and growth form Small to medium-sized herbaceous perennials.

Persistence ✾ ✾ ✾

Fibigias are grey-leaved, yellow-flowered Eurasian perennials with stiffly upright stems followed by tiny, densely packed seedcases, the central grey-pearly septum being the dominant feature, each one being around 10mm long – so resembling a miniature version of honesty

Fibigia clypeata

(*Lunaria annua*). They are particularly good for winter floral arrangements. Full sun and good drainage vital. Z7–9.

Use Good to include in steppe-style or rockery plantings. Effective alongside the smaller ornamental grasses.

Filipendula

ROSACEAE

Size and growth form Large to very large upright clump-forming herbaceous perennials.

Persistence ✿ ✿

Not terribly exciting, but the panicle-form seedheads in combination with the dark brown of the dead leaves provide definite interest in the winter garden. Most species of this moisture-loving genus (found across the Northern Hemisphere) have creamy or pink flowers and divided leaves. Z2–3.

Use Borders, bog gardens, wild gardens (especially on damp soils), meadow and prairie plantings.

Foeniculum vulgare 'Giant Bronze'

Foeniculum Fennel

APIACEAE

Size and growth form Large biennial or short-lived perennial.

Persistence ✿ ✿

Used as a herb as well as a border ornamental, *Foeniculum vulgare* (Z5) makes an attractive border plant with its finely divided foliage and summer-borne yellow flowerheads. Umbel-shaped seedheads then top dark dead stems. A native of drier soils in Europe and west Asia. Perennial in mild winter climates, but apparently only biennial in colder ones.

Use A good, but usually fairly responsible, self-seeder for the border, its matt-textured leaves are an interesting foliage element in summer.

Galtonia

HYACINTHACEAE

Size and growth form Large bulbous perennials.

Persistence ✿ ✿

White flowers in midsummer point downwards, but are followed by upward-pointing seedheads, both heads and stems ghostly pale. Southern African in origin. *G. candicans* is Z5.

Use Generally grown as a border plant; best in a large clump.

Geum Prairie smoke

ROSACEAE

Size and growth form The species discussed is a medium-sized herbaceous perennial.

Persistence ✵✵

Ferny leaves and small pinky-cream flowers make *Geum triflorum* (Z1) a quiet plant in flower, but the immensely fluffy seedheads on 40cm stems in midsummer suddenly draw attention to it. A native of the drier side of the North American prairies.

Use Front of border, rockery, or as part of a short-grass prairie planting.

Glaucium Horned poppy

PAPAVERACEAE

Size and growth form Medium-sized biennials.

Persistence ✵

Bright orange or yellow flowers in summer are followed by unusual very elongated and narrow seedpods. The silvery-grey foliage is quite a feature in its own right. From seashore and dry habitats in Europe, North Africa and west Asia. Z7.

Use Invaluable if you do have to garden by the sea, or in other open dry places. Also good in gravel gardens.

Gleditsia

CAESALPINIACEAE

Size and growth form Deciduous trees.

Persistence ✵✵✵

Pinnate leaves with good yellow autumn colour and inconspicuous flowers followed by the largest seedpods of any frost-hardy plant. North American *G. triacanthos* (Z3) is the only one common in cultivation, and has particularly massive pods, up to 40cm long and 6cm wide, dark brown and flattened. A fine specimen tree, growing to 30 x 20m.

Use Most effective on its own. Deservedly popular for medium-sized and urban gardens.

Glycyrrhiza Liquorice

PAPILIONACEAE

Size and growth form Species discussed are large to very large herbaceous perennials.

Persistence ✵✵/✵✵✵

G. glabra, the source of liquorice (derived from the taproot), has pinnate leaves and pale blue pea-flowers in spikes in late summer, followed

Glaucium flavum

Glycyrrhiza yunnanensis

by far more interesting seedpods – quite unique, being around 2cm across, honey-brown and so difficult to describe that it's easier just to look at the photograph. This species is from Europe and west Asia, but the Chinese *G. yunnanensis* has an almost shrub-like bulk and character. Both are Z8.

Use Possibly too big and scruffy for all but the largest borders. Wild gardens.

Gunnera

GUNNERACEAE

Size and growth form Species discussed are very large herbaceous perennials.

Persistence ❄❄

As befits the all-round extraordinary nature of the vast *G. manicata*, the fruiting bodies have plenty of character – tiny bright orange fruit crowd around fat green cone-shaped stems, which in turn mass on to spikes which can grow to 2m. There must be hundreds of thousands of the fruit on each spike.

Species and varieties *G. manicata* is the commonly seen one, often 3m high and wide; *G. tinctoria* is half the size. A confined root run will effectively 'bonsai' them, although they will never make window-box plants. Both are from South America, and Z7.

Use A classic for waterside locations in big landscapes. Rather overwhelms anything else visually and, indeed, often physically too.

Gypsophila

CARYOPHYLLACEAE

Size and growth form Species discussed are medium to large clump-forming herbaceous perennials.

Persistence ❄❄

A group of plants from Eurasia mostly inhabiting seasonally dry habitats, with white flowers on multi-branched heads in early summer. Winter interest lies in the pale heads. All are long-lived plants, but only on well-drained soils.

Species and varieties *G. paniculata* (Z4) is a bulky perennial (to 1.2m high and wide) with clouds of white flowers which can, given a dry

Gunnera tinctoria

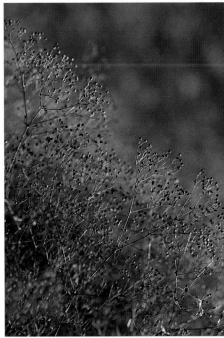

Gypsophila paniculata

autumn, turn into a bleached skeletal mass of intricately branched stems. *G. altissima* does likewise, but vertically (to 1.6m).
Use Adding structural interest to the winter border or dry habitat planting.

Helleborus

RANUNCULACEAE

Size and growth form Small to medium clump-forming herbaceous perennials.
Persistence ✳
Adored by gardeners for their winter flowers, these woodland-edge plants of Europe and western Asia beg a question – if they flowered in June, would we bother growing them? We probably would, at least the *H. x hybridus* group (Z4), as few other flowers display such a proliferation of spotted forms and unusual colours such as slaty-purples, greys and so on. Other species tend to have white or green flowers. All have interesting foliage, effectively evergreen. The nice fat seedpods just ask to be emptied and have their contents grown on, perhaps in the hope of producing a plant that will make all the winter garden visitors go: 'Wow! Where did you get that?'
Use Seedheads are early and short-lived –

generally gone by midsummer – but can look interesting alongside aquilegias and early-flowering geraniums in lightly shaded spots.

Heracleum Hogweed

APIACEAE

Size and growth form Species discussed are large or very large biennials.
Persistence ✳✳/✳✳✳
Impressively large umbellifers for those with space. Creamy white heads in early summer are followed by large seedheads whose skeletons remain until well into the winter.
Species and varieties Few plants have attracted the notoriety of the giant hogweed, *H. mantegazzianum*, both for its aggressive spread through self-seeding and the nasty chemical burns it can cause to the skin if touched during periods of hot weather. Originally from the Caucasus, it became popular as a landscape plant in central Europe during the twentieth century, as well as a fodder plant in some alpine peasant communities, swine at least being happy to eat it. At 3m it is certainly magnificent, in a big enough, or surreal enough, setting. However, given its aggressive seeding, it should be placed where there is no chance of its spreading into wild habitats or of its being accidentally touched. An ideal plant for the gothic garden.

Originating in central Asia, *H. lehmanniana* is sometimes touted as a respectable alternative, but it is smaller (2m) and lacks the impact. The common European wild *H. spondylium* is quite honestly better. *Angelica ursina*, in a different genus altogether, might be the best alternative.
Use For wild-garden settings.

Hordeum Wild barley

POACEAE

Size and growth form Small short-lived perennial grasses.
Persistence ✳✳
The highly distinctive flower- and seedheads of these grasses immediately announce their

relationship to barley – the long extended hair-like awns just ask to be stroked. The heads are, however, sticky, as they are designed by nature to attach themselves to animal fur and so get transported; generations of schoolchildren have discovered this trick and those with curly hair may grow to curse these plants. *H. jubatum* (Z5) is the best known but can self-sow to weed-like proportions on the dry light soils it likes best.
Use Very attractive in low dry plantings, but only suitable for wild-garden situations where its spreading habits will not be a problem.

Hosta

HOSTACEAE

Size and growth form Medium to large herbaceous perennials.
Persistence ✳✳
Originally from the Far East, where the Japanese first began selecting individual plants for their foliage, hostas are grown primarily for the endless variation in their broad leaves. The seedheads which follow the pale mauve flowers are quietly interesting, with downward-pointing three-sided capsules open wide, where the black seed stays suspended for some time after opening. Z3.
Use Given their popularity in moist and shaded sites, it would be a shame to ignore, let alone cut off, hosta seedheads. Somewhat ephemeral in appearance, they are most effective massed.

Humulus Hops

CANNABIDACEAE

Size and growth form Large herbaceous climbers.
Persistence ✳✳
Hops are among the very few climbers with interesting seedheads. Coarse foliage covers twining stems, and female plants bear cone-like leafy flowerheads which dry well, regardless of whether or not they have been fertilized. If used as garden plants, they must

opposite Hordeum jubatum

be given plenty of space as they are vigorous.

Species and varieties *H. japonicus* is sometimes grown as a half-hardy annual for temporary screening. *H. lupulus*, the beer-makers' hop, will climb to 6m in one season, and has straw-coloured female flower- and seedheads, which in Europe are frequently picked and dried and used to decorate bars.

Use Their rapid herbaceous growth makes hops good for summer-only screening, which may be decorative or practical, as in the growing practice of 'façade-greening', the use of large climbers for shading purposes on buildings. Along with vines, they are particularly effective grown over pergolas for shading seating areas.

Hydrangea

HYDRANGEACEAE

Size and growth form Medium to large shrubs.

Persistence ❄ ❄ ❄

Hydrangeas are something of a peripheral subject for this book, as it is the dried flowers that are the main focus of post-floral interest. Those which produce only sterile florets (the so-called 'mopheads') maintain a certain faded glory, whereas those that have an inner zone of tiny fertile florets form genuine seedheads with a more delicate and lacy appearance; both have value for the winter garden. Hydrangeas thrive on moist soils, on acidic ones particularly, often doing well in mild coastal locations. The genus is found naturally in both North America and east Asia.

Species and varieties White-flowered *H. paniculata* 'Floribunda' (Z4) is one of the most magnificent of the genus, with huge (40 x 20cm) heads composed of a mix of sterile florets and seedheads.

H. arborescens 'Annabelle' (Z4) is a white-flowered mophead whose large head combined with smaller than average florets gives it a more aristocratic appearance than the others. The pale brown 'deadheads' make a considerable impact in the winter garden.

Use Doing better in light shade than many shrubs, they are good woodland-edge plants.

Hydrangea macrophylla 'Altona'

Iris pseudacorus

Iris

IRIDACEAE

Size and growth form Species discussed are medium-sized clump-forming herbaceous perennials.

Persistence ✷✷✷

Certain irises in cultivation have fat capsules which stand well amidst the slowly collapsing vegetation around them. The 'bearded' irises popular for their highly ornamental early summer flowers produce little in the way of seedhead interest, however. Irises are found in a wide range of habitats across the northern hemisphere.

Species and varieties *I. sibirica* (Z3) is an incredibly versatile and ecologically tolerant plant which can be relied upon for well-displayed seedheads on stiffly upright stems in both moist and 'average' soil conditions. It is found naturally in marshes across temperate-zone Eurasia.

A variety of species can be found in wetland habitats in both Eurasia and North America, most of which tend to have fat and fairly persistent seedpods, e.g. *I. pseudacorus*, *I. versicolor*, *I. virginica*.

Iris foetidissima (Z6), however, is a real oddity, the only member of the genus to produce berries, which it displays all winter long in rows inside the pod-like seedhead, a good companion to the sturdy dark evergreen leaves. Except that they are not really berries at all, but large seeds with an orange coat.

As if to show that you cannot have everything in life, the flowers are distinctly small and muddy. There are also white-seeded and yellow-seeded cultivars – 'Fructo Albo' and 'Golden Seeded' respectively.

Use The seedheads of moisture-loving species add interest to the often rather dull appearance of waterside environments in winter. *Iris foetidissima* is invaluable for bringing colour to winter borders, particularly those which are somewhat shaded, and the fact that the plant is evergreen is an extra bonus.

Leuzea centaurioides

Liatris scariosa

Jeffersonia

BERBERIDACEAE

Size and growth form Medium-sized herbaceous perennials.

Persistence ✿ ✿

J. diphylla (Z5) is a woodland plant of the eastern USA, with tiny flowers and rather impressive butterfly-shaped leaves.

The seedpod is quite extraordinary, and I can do no better than quote from a colleague, William Cullina, writing in *The New England Wildflower Society Guide to Growing and Propagating Wildflowers of the US and Canada*. He describes the pods as looking 'like a hinged trash can with a lid' which, when squeezed, disgorges the seeds 'like a choking Pac Man just given the Heimlich maneuver'.

Use An effective and good-looking ground cover with the seedheads an added curiosity.

Koelreuteria

SAPINDACEAE

Size and growth form Small trees.

Persistence ✿ ✿ ✿

Grown primarily for their divided foliage and showy yellow flowers, the seedpods of koelreuterias are attractive too, the bladder-type capsules resembling Chinese lanterns, containing hard seeds which have been used for beads. East Asia. Z7.

Use Growing to only 9m, they are good trees for smaller gardens.

Lagurus Hare tail

POACEAE

Size and growth form Medium-sized annual grass.

Persistence ✿ ✿ ✿

Off-white to grey fluffy heads of a vaguely triangular shape which stand firmly upright. Distinctly tactile. Particularly suitable for drying. Mediterranean in origin.

Use For combining with annual flowers and other annual grasses.

Leuzea

ASTERACEAE

Size and growth form Large to very large herbaceous perennials.

Persistence ✿ ✿

Resembling smaller versions of the globe artichoke *Cynara cardunculus*, leuzeas have similar chunky purple flowers and seedheads. Mediterranean region. Z6.

Use An underrated plant for large borders or wild gardens, particularly for drier locations.

Liatris

ASTERACEAE

Size and growth form Medium-sized clump-forming herbaceous perennials

Persistence ✿ ✿

The distinct spike shape adopted by the flower- and seedheads of some liatris species makes an interesting contrast to looser forms around them. Most species have pink flowers in mid- to late summer. All are from North America, generally frequenting drier habitats. Most are Z3.

Use Borders and prairie habitat plantings.

111

Ligularia hodgsonii

Ligularia

ASTERACEAE

Size and growth form Large clump-forming herbaceous perennials.

Persistence ✹✹

Typical fluffy daisy-family seed is carried on heads of various shapes. All are large plants of luxuriant appearance and Eurasian origin, with yellow flowers in midsummer. *L. stenocephala* (Z5) is the most outstanding of the species commonly available in seed, with 2m-tall narrow spires with large (2cm wide) bunches of pale downward-pointing seed. *L. fischeri* is similar, but at around a third taller, is a particularly dramatic plant. Those with flowers in bunches, such as *L. hodgsonii* (Z5), are less striking but still worthwhile.

Use Make a great impact in large-scale plantings on moist soil.

Lilium Lily

LILIACEAE

Size and growth form Border species are medium-sized to large bulbous perennials.

Persistence ✹✹✹

Upright stems bear flowers in a great variety of colours and shapes. Fat, rounded pods hold on for some time after their plentiful seed is released. There are a great many lily species from a variety of habitats throughout the cooler zones of the Northern Hemisphere.

Use The fact that the showy flowers are followed by such good seedheads adds to their value as border plants. Lilies are among the few common container plants to have attractive seedheads. Some, such as *L. martagon* (Z3), do well in light shade and woodland-edge settings.

Limonium Sea-lavender

PLUMBAGINACEAE

Size and growth form The species discussed is a small to medium-sized clump-forming herbaceous perennial.

Persistence ✹✹

Balkan *L. latifolium* (Z3) is the most commonly grown of a varied genus. It has heads of intricately branching stems with masses of tiny lavender-coloured flowers followed by equally tiny seedheads – the impact is mostly from the branching stems. Glossy leaves add to a long-season appeal. Flourishes by the coast and on dry soils.

Use Best for open border plantings on dry soils or in gravel gardens.

opposite Limonium platyphyllum 'Blue Diamond'

Lunaria Honesty

BRASSICACEAE

Size and growth form Medium-sized clump-forming herbaceous perennials and biennials.

Persistence ✳ ✳
Among the most distinctive of all 'seedyhead' plants, with the pearly septum between the two halves of the capsule shining positively silver in winter sunlight.

Species and varieties *L. annua* is a biennial with particularly large glistening seed capsules, at least once the outer walls have fallen off. This characteristic, along with the springtime deep pink flowers and happily self-sowing habit, have made it a popular cottage-garden plant. It can also naturalize in light shade.
L. rediviva is a soundly perennial species with much smaller seedheads. Its sweetly scented pale pink flowers are borne for several months in spring. Both originate in Europe. Both Z4.

Use Borders and wild gardens in sun or light shade.

Lupinus

PAPILIONACEAE

Size and growth form Species discussed are medium to large biennials and short-lived herbaceous perennials.

Persistence ✳ ✳
Bright early summer flowers are followed by distinctive upright heads of long thin pods. A varied North American genus, all with attractive palmate leaves. There are innumerable hybrids in a very wide range of colours and a goodly number of species, most of them blue or violet. The plants' seedheads make an impact *en masse*, although they tend to look scruffy at close quarters. Z3.

Use The hybrids are classic 'olde-worlde' border plants, their upright shape being echoed by hollyhocks and mulleins (*Verbascum* species) for an Alice in Wonderland touch.

Lunaria rediviva

Lysimachia

PRIMULACEAE

Size and growth form Species discussed are medium-sized clump-forming herbaceous perennials, often with strong spreading tendencies.

Persistence ✹✹

A genus of, generally, extremely vigorous plants, with white or yellow flowers. Iberian early- to midsummer flowering *L. ephemerum* (Z7) is the only one with much post-flowering impact – narrow spikes of small white flowers above grey foliage. The seedheads make a useful vertical accent.

Use Borders or wild gardens, including those in light shade.

Lythrum Purple loosestrife

LYTHRACEAE

Size and growth form Species discussed are large clump-forming herbaceous perennials.

Lythrum

Persistence ✹✹✹

Easy versatile perennials with pink flowers in spikes in midsummer – a good many such spikes per plant can be produced, giving the flowers considerable impact. Physically strong winter stems with small seed capsules.

Species and varieties There are two similar species in cultivation, *L. salicaria* and *L. virgatum*, the latter being somewhat more elegant in appearance. Their cultivation in North America is to be discouraged, as these Eurasian species have proved to be extremely invasive in wetland habitats. Both Z3.

Use Suitable for both waterside and other moist environments and ordinary border conditions. The stiff uprights of the stems complement grasses well.

Malva

MALVACEAE

Size and growth form The species discussed is a medium-sized short-lived perennial.

Persistence ✹✹

M. moschata (Z3) has pink flowers in early summer and very divided palmate foliage with 'pie-like' seedheads similar to *Alcea*. Native to Europe, there are several other similar species.

Use For both borders and wildflower meadows.

Matteuccia

DRYOPTERIDACEAE

Size and growth form Medium-sized spreading deciduous ferns.

Persistence ✹✹

One of the few deciduous ferns to have much winter impact, *M. struthiopteris* (Z2) has upright bunches of brown spore-bearing fronds. Found across the Northern Hemisphere.

Use Needs a moist soil, so often planted in waterside or moist-shade environments. Best *en masse*, which it does by itself, as it has a suckering habit.

Melica

POACEAE

Size and growth form Medium-sized herbaceous perennial grasses.

Persistence ✹/✹✹

The various species of *Melica* are delightful but have among the shortest period of interest of all the grasses. Only *M. transsilvanica* and *M. ciliata* (both Z5) last into early autumn. Both are species from dry and steppe habitats in central and eastern Europe, with fluffy cylindrical pale straw-coloured heads. Good on dry alkaline soils.

Use A fine companion for early- to midsummer-flowering dry-meadow flowers like *Dianthus carthusianorum* and *Salvia nemorosa*.

Miscanthus Eulalia grass

POACEAE

Size and growth form Medium-sized to large herbaceous perennial grasses.

Persistence ✹✹✹

M. sinensis (Z4) and a number of other similar species from east Asia are the source of a large, and constantly expanding, range of resilient and reliable ornamental grasses. The flowers are borne in late summer or autumn and can be anything from silver to grey, to pink or brown, but these inevitably turn duller as the winter proceeds. Physically, however, they stand winter well, making them possibly the most important group of seedhead plants. All thrive on fertile soil. Full sun is advised, but most cultivars will give good results on sites which do not receive sun all day. Growth starts relatively early in the year, even in cooler climates.

When considering miscanthus it is advisable to get a feel for the characteristics of different varieties. Size varies enormously, from 1.6 to 3m. The way that the flower- and seedheads are displayed can vary greatly too, from those such as 'Red Star' which are too densely packed to appreciate, to the very upright, impressive, but rather graceless 'Rotsilber' and 'Hermann Müssel'.

opposite *Miscanthus sinensis* 'Flamingo'

M. sinensis cultivars and hybrids	Award	Height	Flower colour	Notes
'Adagio'		1.5m	beige	compact, narrow foliage
var. *condensatus* 'Cosmopolitan'	AM	2m	copper red	upright
'Ferner Osten'		1.8m	very dark red	good autumn colour
'Flamingo'	AM	2m	dark pink	upright, good autumn colour
'Gewitterwolke'	AM	1.8m	dark pink	upright
'Ghana'	AM	1.6m	red-brown	red-orange autumn colour, less vigorous
'Grosse Fontäne'	AM	2.4m	silver-red	slightly pendent seedheads
'Kaskade'	AM	2m	pink	slightly pendent seedheads, narrow upright habit
'Kleine Silberspinne'	AM	1.5m	silky red	compact growth
'Morning Light'	AM	1.6m	pinkish	very elegant habit
'Professor Richard Hansen'		2m	red-pink	creamy seedheads held well clear of foliage
'Roland'		2.4m	pinkish	very statuesque
'Septemberrot'	AM	2.4m	reddish	broad foliage
'Silberfeder'	AM	2m	silvery	upright habit, silvery seedheads
'Strictus'	AM	1.8m	pink-red	variegated foliage, upright
'Undine'	AM	2m	pinky mauve	fluffy seedheads, upright
'Yakushima Dwarf'		1.4–1.6m	buff-cream	very compact
'Zwergelefant'		2.2m	silvery red	'crimped' appearance to flower-/seedheads
M. nepalensis		1.5m	cream	airy seedheads, long-lasting and very good

Miscanthus 'Flammenmeer'

Miscanthus sinensis 'Juli'

Miscanthus sinensis 'Gearmella'

In warm temperate or Mediterranean climates, *Miscanthus* can seed profusely, and consequently are to be regarded as a potentially invasive alien.

Species and varieties A comprehensive list would be out of date as soon as it was published; instead, I have simply listed those which have received an Award of Merit from the Royal Horticultural Society following several years of trials in southern England which do have good seedheads, plus a couple of other notably good cultivars. Flower colours are given; as a general rule they fade as the seed ripens so that winter colours are a more uniform silvery-beige/soft brown, with only a memory of the more vivid floral shades.

Use *Miscanthus* have stature and delicacy, and as such are very valuable decorative elements. They are perhaps most useful when combined with herbaceous plants of around half to three-quarters their height; companions any taller somewhat reduce the impact of the *Miscanthus*. The tallest varieties are highly effective used with prairie and other tall perennials. Shorter varieties are often more appropriate in smaller gardens and plantings. All varieties have great impact both at a distance and at close hand.

One of the great joys of *Miscanthus* is the way the plumes of their flower- and seedheads all point the same way in a breeze. Not for nothing does the plant frequently feature in traditional Japanese nature paintings. This habit reminds many of reeds, and points to a useful aspect of the plant, which is to evoke reeds and other waterside vegetation to create context in plantings around artificial ponds, where it is impossible to establish genuine marginal vegetation, as the soil is not moist enough.

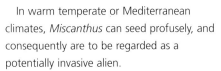

Molinia caerulea

M. caerulea cultivars	Height	Flower-/seedhead colour	Notes
'Dauerstrahl'	90cm	dark	stiffly upright
'Edith Dudszus'	90cm	dark	upright
'Heidebraut'	1.2m	straw colour	relatively persistent in winter
'Moorflamme'	1m	dark purple autumn colour, orange in winter	
'Moorhexe'	1m	dark	stiffly upright
'Poul Petersen'	60cm	yellow-orange	compact
'Strahlenquelle'	1.2m	purplish	dramatic arching habit
M.c. subsp. arundinacea cultivars:			
'Bergfreund'	1.5m	strong yellow	
'Fontäne'	1.8m	dark	arching habit
'Karl Foerster'	2.2m	golden brown turning yellow,	upright
'Skyracer'	2.4m	golden yellow	good autumn colour
'Transparent'	2.2m	purplish turning orange-brown,	standing longer than others
'Windsaule'	2.5m	orange-yellow	more delicate in appearance than others
'Windspiel'	2m	honey colour	seedheads always in motion

Molinia

POACEAE

Size and growth form Medium-sized to large herbaceous perennial grasses.

Persistence ❋ ❋

Natives of Eurasia, these are an attractive group of grasses, noted for their ability to thrive on poor soils. Cultivars of *M. caerulea* (Z4) will be particularly suitable for exposed sites with acidic soil; those of the larger *M. caerulea* subsp. *arundinacea* (*M. littoralis*) are better suited to less windy sites; the subspecies is by nature a woodland-edge plant of central and southern Europe, whereas 'straight' *M. caerulea* originates from bleaker northern environments. *Molinia* varieties are more tolerant of a little shade than most grasses.

The stiffly radiating yellow stems of molinias have the quality of the firework about them, with most of the impact being the stem itself rather than the seedhead. Despite the size of some cultivars, they take up little space as their flower- and seedhead stems are relatively upright. Their disadvantage is that they tend to break off at the base by late autumn, although 'Transparent' lasts somewhat longer.
Use Invaluable for herbaceous borders and naturalistic perennial plantings, as they add structure and line to the gradually increasing chaos and dereliction of less rigid autumn perennial growth. The way the stems seem to shoot outwards from the base adds a touch of surprise and drama to borders. The larger *arundinacea* cultivars are particularly valuable for adding height to plantings, as they do without taking up much space at the bottom. Contrasting compact dark seedheads, like those of *Phlomis tuberosa* or monardas, are effective companions.

Molopospermum

APIACEAE

Size and growth form Large perennial.
Persistence ❋ ❋

M. peloponnesiacum is an impressive umbellifer from southern Europe. Shiny, deeply cut foliage and large heads of creamy flowers followed by large seedheads. Seems to be reliably perennial. Sun or light shade.
Use A good companion for woodland-edge perennials – *Astrantia*, *Digitalis*, *Geranium* and so on.

Molopospermum peloponnesiacum

Monarda Bergamot, bee balm

LAMIACEAE

Size and growth form Species discussed are large clump-forming herbaceous perennials.

Persistence ❋❋/❋❋❋

Immensely useful for their midsummer flowers, with hybrids in shades of pink to mauve and violet, plus some good scarlets and whites, monardas are also valuable for winter structure – tight whorls of seed capsules scattered up the upright stems having more persistence than those of many flowering perennials. The garden hybrids are descended from species of prairie and woodland-edge habitats in North America. Z4.

Use Good for combining with grasses and other fuzzy 'soft-definition' plants.

Morina

MORINACEAE

Size and growth form Medium-sized herbaceous perennials.

Persistence ❋❋❋

Thistle-like bracts surround most unthistly small pinky-white tubular flowers in early summer. The bracts remain around the seedheads, turning a silvery grey. Spiny leaves add to the general thistle-like appearance. West Asian semi-desert origin. Hardy, but good drainage essential. Most Z6.

Use Unusual plants for the front of the border or dry-habitat plantings.

Nectaroscordum

LILIACEAE

Size and growth form Large bulbous perennials.

Persistence ❋❋

N. siculum (Z7) is an allium relative with nodding flowers in a very muddy shade of pink, which does not seem to stop people growing it. The conical seedheads, by contrast, stand pertly upright and have real character. Originally from south-east Europe and west Asia.

Use In borders, but can be naturalized in grass.

opposite *Monarda* 'Aquarius' with *Cornus florida rubra* 'Cherokee' behind

Morina

Nicandra

SOLANACEAE

Size and growth form Large annual.
Persistence ❆❆

Peruvian *N. physalodes* (Z8) (shoofly plant) is an annual with a branching habit, tending to spread out as wide as it grows tall. Purple flowers produce berries, which are concealed in lantern-shaped pale green calyces, maturing to fawn.

Use An effective member of summer plantings which stress the large, tropical and robust, alongside other large annuals such as *Ricinus communis*, *Cleome hassleriana* and *Nicotiana* species.

Nigella

RANUNCULACEAE

Size and growth form Small to medium-sized annuals.
Persistence ❆❆

The pink and blue flowers of the commonly grown forms of *N. damascena* are followed by distinctive inflated seedpods around 1.5cm long, each one topped by several 'horns'.

A native of the warmer parts of Europe and west Asia, it has been long popular as a cottage-garden flower (known commonly as 'love-in-a-mist'), and the black seeds are used as a spice in south Asian cuisine, mainly for flavouring flatbreads. Called 'kalonji' in Hindi/Urdu, they are sometimes mistakenly called 'onion seed' in English.

N. hispanica has a narrower seedhead with 'horns' which stretch out more dramatically. *N. arvensis* has seedheads which are narrower still.

Use Cottage garden and other informal annual plantings.

Onoclea

ATHYRIACEAE

Size and growth form Medium-sized spreading herbaceous fern.
Persistence ❆❆❆

O. sensibilis (Z4) is a native of damp areas in eastern North America and east Asia. Its upright fronds, coarsely divided but still elegant, emerge from a strongly running rootstock. Spores are borne on separate fertile fronds, which lack any green matter but

instead are covered in black bead-like structures that contain the spores. These strange structures persist well through the winter.

Use The running habit makes it suitable only for large bog gardens or damp prairie plantings, where competition from other species will stand up to it and reduce its vigour.

Paeonia Peony

PAEONIACEAE

Size and growth form The species mentioned is a large herbaceous perennial.
Persistence ❆

P. mlokosewitschii (Z6) from the Caucasus is the only peony commonly grown with distinctive seedheads, or more correctly seeds, these being an exuberant bright pink, displayed in rows in the open seedpods for several weeks in midsummer, somewhat longer than the nine-day wonder of the pale yellow flowers. The fresh green rounded foliage is nice, though.

Use Adds stature and interest to permanent herbaceous plantings.

Nigella

Paeonia mlokosewitschii

Panicum Switch grass

POACEAE

Size and growth form Large to very large herbaceous perennial grasses.

Persistence ✹ ✹ ✹

A classic North American prairie grass, *P. virgatum* (Z4), known as switch grass, has extremely delicate flowerheads in late summer, maturing to equally airy seedheads. The autumn colour of several cultivars is also a notable feature, as is their upright habit, which makes them good border plants. Full sunlight is essential, as well as an absence of competition from neighbouring species which make early growth; in climates with a long, relatively cool growing season, *Panicum* is one of the last ornamental grasses to start growing, and it is all too easily crowded out by the vigorous growth of other herbaceous plants.

This increasingly widely grown hardy ornamental grass is only one of a great many species, mostly tropical. Of these, millet, *P. miliaceum*, is a food crop of vital importance to many developing world farmers. It has a form 'Purpureum' with purple-flushed foliage

Species and varieties

P. virgatum cultivars	Height	Leaf colour/autumn colour	Notes
'Cloud Nine'	2.2m	blue-green, turning yellow	upright habit
'Dallas Blues'	1.6m	blue-toned foliage	
'Hänse Herms'	1.2m	reddish in summer, turning burgundy	abundant flower/seed panicles
'Heavy Metal'	1.2m	grey-blue,	very upright
'Northwind'	2m	blue-grey, turning orange-yellow	
'Prairie Sky'	1.2m	blue-toned	relaxed habit, good
'Rehbraun'	1.2m	green, turning orange, red	
'Shenandoah'	1.2m	red tones, turning burgundy	

Panicum

Panicum virgatum 'Rehbraun'

and large fluffy flower-/seedheads which is sometimes grown as an ornamental.

Use Combines well with medium-sized or larger perennials, the light heads a contrast to heavier forms. Not particularly effective at long distance. An important component in prairie-style plantings.

Papaver Poppy

PAPAVERACEAE

Size and growth form Small to medium-sized annuals and herbaceous perennials.

Persistence ✳✳
The 'salt-shaker' heads of poppies are among the most easily recognizable of all seedheads. The species in cultivation originate from southern Europe and west Asia.

Species and varieties
Perennial *P. orientale* (Z3) and its hybrids, with their showy pink, red and orange flowers, are relatively early-flowering as border plants go, so their pods are mature by midsummer. Possibly best appreciated dried in winter arrangements.

Annual *P. somniferum* (Z7), the opium poppy, has the largest flowers and the most distinctive seedpods, which are inflated to the point of almost being spherical, with a distinctive cap-like top. Raw opium is produced from the sides of the unripe capsule. The seed (which contains next to none of the drug) is used extensively in the making of bread and cakes in European cuisine. A classic cottage-garden annual.

Use The annual varieties are effective in informal summer plantings, the perennial *P. orientale* group in herbaceous plantings, where its early season makes it particularly valued.

Pastinacea Wild parsnip

APIACEAE

Size and growth form Species discussed is a large herbaceous biennial.

Persistence
P. sativa is a fresh green plant with yellow-green flowers in mid- to late summer. Seedheads are of medium size for an umbellifer and attractively chunky, making a good contrast to the finer ones of carrots.

Use Wild parsnip is found in a range of habitats in northern and central Europe, making it a valuable constituent of wildflower meadow mixes, especially those for poorer soils.

In border cultivation, parsnips can become ridiculously tall, and out of scale with shorter plants. A better effect can be achieved if shop-bought parsnips are planted out in the garden instead, as they do not grow so tall.

Pennisetum Fountain grass

POACEAE

Size and growth form Medium-sized herbaceous perennial grasses.

Persistence ✳✳/✳✳✳
'Fluffiness' just has to be the first word that comes to mind when faced with the majority of *Pennisetum* species. Mid- to late summer flowers give way to seedheads whose effect is magnified by their being so profuse. Some are low-growing, making them ideal for a wide range of garden situations.

All need good drainage, and in climates where winters are wet plants will often not survive in clay soils or any others where drainage is less than perfect; in addition they definitely seem better suited to continental rather than

Papaver somniferum

Pastinacea

maritime climates. One reason for this is that they need heat to start growing, and so can make a late start in cool summer climates.
Species and varieties The hardier species, a selection of which is discussed in the table, are generally of Asian origin. However, the genus is widely distributed throughout the tropics, and some of these are now making an appearance in temperate-zone gardens as seasonal bedding plants. Among them is the 1.2m high *P. macrostachyum* 'Burgundy Giant', with dark red-brown foliage and huge maize-like heads of silky pink. *P. glaucum* 'Purple Majesty' is similar, but coarser. *P. setaceum* 'Rubrum' has red foliage, and red flowers which fade to fawn seedheads.

Pennisetum is a genus with considerable appeal, and excellent new varieties appear annually – some of them noted for their small size. However, it may take years to establish just how reliable they are as garden plants.
Use Pennisetums are effective both close to and, if used generously, at a distance. Their relatively low height makes them particularly useful for front-of-border positions in lower herbaceous plantings, and the lowest varieties are especially

Pennisetum	Height	Flower-/seedheads	Other characteristics
P. alopecuroides			Z6
P.a. 'Cassian's Choice'	1m	light brown	rich orange foliage in autumn
P.a. 'Hameln'	60cm	golden in autumn	
P.a. 'Woodside'	70cm	beige-cream	selected for early flowering
P.a. f. *viridescens*	1m	very dark brown	also known as 'Moudry'
P. orientale	60cm	pinky-cream	Z7
P. thunbergii 'Red Buttons'	1m	tight mid-brown heads, turning white	hardiness not established
P. villosum	60cm	very furry, white	Z9

Pennisetum alopecuroides 'Cassian's Choice'

Pennisetum orientale 'Shogun'

effective along paths. Mass plantings can be spectacular, as James van Sweden and Wolfgang Oehme have shown in numerous situations on the US East Coast. They are very effective when used as a foreground for compositions of taller herbaceous plants, or as a matrix plant to create a meadow-style effect with short to medium-height late-flowering perennials such as species of *Coreopsis*, *Rudbeckia* and *Aster*.

The half-hardy species are highly effective if used in seasonal planting schemes with other annuals or temporary summer plants, and can be seen in both naturalistic and formal schemes. They are also striking in pots.

Perovskia Russian sage

LAMIACEAE

Size and growth form Medium-sized perennial, but with a woody base.

Persistence ❋❋❋

The aromatic foliage and mauve-blue flowers borne in midsummer have made this a popular garden plant, especially for its drought tolerance – it is common throughout the dry regions of central Asia. During winter its insignificant seed capsules dot unusually white stems. Z3.

Use Perovskia's white stems stand out against the generally much darker remains of other perennials.

Phlomis

LAMIACEAE

Size and growth form Medium-sized herbaceous perennials and subshrubs.

Persistence ❋❋❋

The calyces of old phlomis flowers form a hard casing for the seed, making them among the most durable of all seedheads. The fact that they are scattered at intervals up the stem adds to their appeal. Most are from dry habitats in Europe and west Asia.

Species and varieties Most of the species in cultivation are grey-leaved subshrubs, with seedheads on quite bendy stems. *P. italica* (Z8) is useful for combining with other Mediterranean-climate low shrubs in drought-tolerant plantings.

above *Perovskia* opposite *Phlomis russeliana* with *Deschampsia cespitosa* behind

P. russeliana (Z7) is a very distinctive herbaceous species, immensely useful for its weed-suppressing mat of large evergreen leaves, golden flowers in early summer and very persistent large whorls of seed capsules, making it one of the best of all herbaceous plants for winter interest.

P. tuberosa (Z6) has pink flowers in early summer on upright stems, which mature to small whorled seedheads.

Use Invaluable for definition, highly effective against a backdrop of pale and fuzzy grasses, the stiffly upright *P. tuberosa* especially.

Phormium New Zealand flax

PHORMIACEAE

Size and growth form Very large evergreen rosette-forming perennial.

Persistence ✿✿✿

This New Zealand plant is now widely (perhaps too widely) planted for its evergreen strap-shaped leaves. Older plants produce dull red flowers on 4m spikes followed by very dark, upwardly pointing narrow capsules, apparently clawing at the sky with a menacing air. Highly effective, and thoroughly gothic in silhouette. Z8.

Use In danger of becoming a cliché, phormiums grow well by the sea in the company of other salt-resistant exotica like eucalypts and cordylines. Those who site them in narrow borders may well repent, and should remove the plants before earth-moving equipment is needed.

Physalis

SOLANACEAE

Size and growth form Species discussed are medium-sized annuals and herbaceous perennials.

Persistence ✿✿/✿✿✿

Rather coarse leaves and inconspicuous flowers are put in the shade by the unusual papery husk which develops from the calyx and which surrounds the fruit itself, a berry which is generally edible, with a refreshing sour taste. All need fertile soils.

Species and varieties *P. alkekengi* (Z3) is a Eurasian clump-forming herbaceous perennial

with running roots. The common English name 'Chinese lanterns' says it all: dark orange inflated 'pods' shaped like an inverted onion, about 5–6cm long and 5cm wide. Inside are orange berries.

P. peruviana (Z8), known inaccurately as the Cape gooseberry, although it is from South America, is similar, but showier. The pale orange fruit is good to eat.

P. ixocarpa (Z8), Mexican ground cherry or tomatillo, is a medium-sized to large annual species with greeny-yellow calyx. Perennial *P. philadelphica* (Z7), also known as tomatillo, is widely cultivated as a food crop, the purple-black berries being more ornamental than the calyx, from which they tend to burst out.

Use An unusual element in border plantings, adding a welcome exotic touch in late autumn and early winter.

Phytolacca Pokeweed

PHYTOLACCACEAE

Size and growth form The species discussed is a large herbaceous perennial.

Persistence ✿/✿✿

P. americana (Z4) has pink-red berries in tight cylindrical formation, turning inky-black and having a rather sinister appearance (they are poisonous) in autumn and early winter. The flowers are rather inconspicuous, while the foliage is lush but coarse looking. In some gardens it can self-sow and become a nuisance. Fertile soil and happy in light shade. Chinese *P. decandra* is very similar.

Use One of those plants with too coarse an appearance and gawky a manner to be properly ornamental. A curiosity, a wild garden plant, or a denizen of the gothic-style garden.

Pimpinella

APIACEAE

Size and growth form The species discussed is a large perennial.

Persistence ✿✿

Pimpinella major 'Rosea' is a tall but delicate-looking umbellifer with heads of small rounded seeds following pale pink flowers.

Pimpinella major 'Rosea'

A great self-seeder, but so delicate that it rarely becomes a problem.
Use In combination with other wispy and loose wildflowers and perennials.

Podophyllum May apple
BERBERIDACEAE

Size and growth form Small to medium-sized clump-forming herbaceous perennials.
Persistence ✴✴
Large foliage and good-sized solitary flowers in spring are followed in late summer by a single berry 2.5–5cm wide. All need cool woodland conditions.
Species and varieties Fruit is yellow or red in the case of North American *P. peltatum* (Z4); red to purple tones in the two Chinese species *P. difforme* and *P. hexandrum* (Z6).
Use In shaded situations alongside other slow-growing choice forest-floor species.

Proboscidea Devil's claw
PEDALIACEAE

Size and growth form Medium-sized annuals.
Persistence ✴✴
A group of annuals from the warmer parts of the Americas with strange claw-like fruit – hence the common name (and a number of others such as elephant's trunk plant and unicorn plant). The flowers are generally red and purple, followed by the 7–12cm long fruit, which when immature can be pickled and eaten. The plants are frost-tender (Z10) and should be treated as half-hardy.
Use Primarily grown as a curiosity, but the plants are large for an annual – which can make it valuable for seasonal plantings, perhaps alongside *Ricinus*, *Amaranthus* etc.

Pulsatilla Pasque flower
RANUNCULACEAE

Size and growth form Small herbaceous perennials.
Persistence ✴
Among the earliest flowering herbaceous plants for open sunny situations, pulsatillas have showy anemone-like flowers, succeeded

by fluffy seedheads whose similarity to those of clematis betray a botanical relationship which may at first surprise. The seedheads mature at a time (early summer) when much else around them may be in full flower. The finely divided foliage is attractive in its own right. All are plants of well-drained calcareous soils in the Northern Hemisphere. Most Z4–6.
Use Rockeries or wildflower-meadow plantings for dry alkaline soils.

Rhinanthus Yellow rattle
SCROPHULARIACEAE

Size and growth form Small annual.
Persistence ✴✴
As pale yellow flowers dotted through the tight grass of wildflower meadows is how *R. minor*, yellow rattle, is normally seen. It is one of several annual species scattered across the Northern Hemisphere which are semi-parasitic on grass. The seedheads, of this species at least, are comparatively large, up to 1cm across, thin papery brown packets, and quite a feature *en masse*. These plants can play an important part in meadow ecology, as they weaken grasses, so allowing other non-grass species to become more dominant and hence visible. The seed needs to be sown into the meadow in autumn; germination

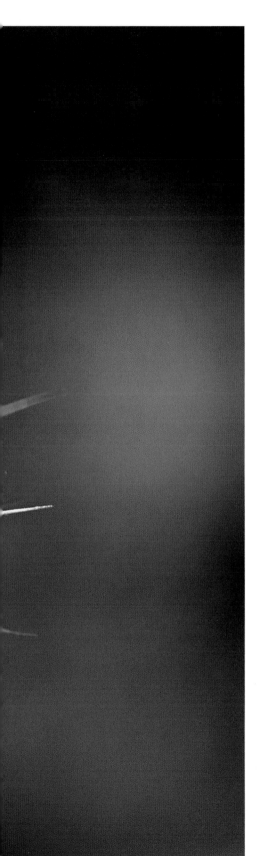
Pulsatilla vulgaris

Rhinanthus

readily follows in spring, and the plant will gradually take hold. In nature, the species are generally found on less fertile soils, but appear to be happy on a range of soils in cultivation.
Use Can be grown only in conjunction with grasses.

Rudbeckia Black-eyed Susan

ASTERACEAE

Size and growth form Species discussed are medium-sized to very large clump-forming herbaceous perennials.

Persistence 🌼🌼

Bold yellow flowers with dark centres make these among the most popular of late-summer and autumn border perennials. The dark cone-shaped seedheads of all have some value, those of the taller species making more impact simply by being higher up and therefore more conspicuous. Most are native to North American prairie environments.

Species and varieties At 2m tall, *R. laciniata* (Z3) is the most dramatic. *R. maxima* (Z7) is also good, both for seedheads and for its glaucous paddle-shaped foliage.

Use First-rate border plants for sun and fertile soils. Prairie plantings.

Rudbeckia species

Salvia Sage

LAMIACEAE

Size and growth form Species discussed are medium-sized herbaceous perennials or biennials.

Persistence 🌼/🌼🌼

A huge genus, spread across the globe, with an enormous range of flower colours, but few have seedheads with enough persistence to mark them out.

Species and varieties *S. farinacea* (Z9) has mealy white stems and tiny seedheads. The various forms of *S. sclarea* (Z9), clary, are distinguished by persistent showy bracts in a variety of colours (everything between blue and dull rosy red). The plant is an annual or biennial growing to 60cm and has a spreading habit. Biennial *S. sclarea* subsp. *turkestanica* is taller (to 1m) and has very distinctive off-white bracts flushed mauve.

Use In combination with other annuals or biennials. *S. sclarea* is particularly effective in conjunction with *Achillea*, *Verbascum*, *Knautia* and other *Salvia* species in plantings on dry calcareous soils.

Sanguisorba

ROSACEAE

Size and growth form Medium to large clump-forming herbaceous perennials.

Persistence 🌼🌼

Sanguisorbas are mostly plants of damp soils, with species scattered across the Northern Hemisphere. Their foliage is divided into leaflets and is always attractive. Flowers and seeds are carried on tight heads which sit atop upright and often much-branched stems.

Species and varieties *S. officinalis* (Z5) and *S. tenuifolia* (Z4) have the tightest and neatest heads, which look good in silhouette against a light background. The airy multi-branched stems allow you to look through them, effectively making the plants 'transparent'.

Use The seedheads add definition to combinations of grasses and other perennials.

Scabiosa

DIPSACACEAE

Size and growth form The species discussed is a medium-sized annual.

Persistence ✳✳

Found wild around the southern and eastern shores of the Mediterranean, *S. prolifera*, Carmel daisy, has cream flowers which leave behind a very distinctive round seedhead, about 3cm across, vaguely reminiscent of either a Sputnik or a lighting installation in a 1960s hotel.

Use A curiosity for the annual border. Good for drying.

Schizachyrium Little bluestem

POACEAE

Size and growth form Medium to large herbaceous perennial grass.

Persistence ✳✳/✳✳✳

S. scoparium (Z3) is one of the most important constituents of the North American prairie. Its fluffy heads of seed catch the autumn light beautifully, but even as these release their seed, the plants look very ornamental until late winter because of the strong bronze to orange shade of their dead leaves and stems. In northern Europe the plants can be short-lived.

Use In prairie and other wild-style plantings. Has border potential, although in warmer climates its vigorous self-seeding habit may be a nuisance. Good companion for *Miscanthus*, *Panicum*, *Molinia* and other larger grasses.

Scutellaria

LAMIACEAE

Size and growth form Small to medium-sized clump-forming herbaceous perennials.

Persistence ✳✳

North American *S. incana* (Z5) has attractive blue-mauve flowers in early summer followed by very pale, almost ghostly, little seedheads on fine stems, best seen against a dark background. Dutch writer Henk Gerritsen once likened them to miniature baseball caps.

Use Adds structure to plantings in light shade. Particularly effective with geranium species.

Sedum

CRASSULACEAE

Size and growth form Species discussed are medium-sized herbaceous perennials.

Persistence ✳✳✳

S. spectabile and *S. telephium* have given rise to a number of hybrids all with very characteristic pale green fleshy leaves and umbel-shaped flowerheads in late summer in shades of pink, dull red and cream. After flowering some colour lasts for a while, but eventually only a dark brown seedhead is left, whose persistence makes it very useful for the winter border. Originating from dry-meadow environments in Eurasia, these plants thrive in full sun and have good drought tolerance. Z3.

Use Classic front-of-border plants, but also popular for mass-planting owing to the fact that they never look untidy. They add interest to dry-habitat plantings, and are of particular value here for their late flowering.

Sanguisorba 'Blackthorn'

Sedum spectabile 'Indian Chief' with *Calamagrostis* behind

Senna

FABACEAE

Size and growth form The species discussed
is a large to very large herbaceous perennial.

Persistence ❋ ❋

Golden yellow flowers in late summer and
impressive divided foliage make *S. hebecarpa*
(Z5) well worth growing. Long thin pods in
autumn belie the distant relationship to beans.
Native to central and eastern USA.

Use In prairie or wild plantings. Effective in the
border alongside other large late perennials
like eupatoriums, asters and vernonias.

Serratula

ASTERACEAE

Size and growth form Clump-forming
perennial herbaceous plants.

Persistence ❋

An underrated genus of very late-flowering
plants. Only *S. tinctoria* (Z6) is at all widely
grown. Metre-high stems support purple-pink
flowers, followed by fluffy aster-like
seedheads.

Use Valuable for autumn borders.

Sisyrinchium

IRIDACEAE

Size and growth form Species discussed is
a medium-sized clump-forming perennial.

Persistence ❋ ❋

S. striatum (Z8) has iris-like foliage and pale
yellow flowers in whorls on 70cm stems,
followed by similarly bunched seedheads.

Use This plant often self-sows vigorously,
particularly in paving and gravel gardens, and
the repetition of its seedheads across space
can make a striking winter impression.

Smilacina False Solomon's seal

LILIACEAE

Size and growth form Medium-sized clump-
forming perennials.

Persistence ❋ ❋

A North American genus which needs a cool

Solidago cutleri 'September Gold'

shady site, this is another group of woodland
plants with berries. *S. racemosa* (Z4) is the
most commonly grown, with short-lived white
flowers in spring and rather elegant broad
foliage. Its berries start off white, but turn
gradually to red. Less striking in flower and
foliage is *S. stellata* (Z3), but this has marble-
sized berries which go from pale green through
a red pattern and finally end up dark red.

Use A good accompaniment to other
woodlanders like arisaemas and trilliums.

Solidago Goldenrod

ASTERACEAE

Size and growth form Large to very large
clump-forming perennials, some with a
running habit.

Persistence ❋ ❋

Goldenrods are still in the process of being
'rehabilitated', recovering their image as plants
worth growing from decades when they were
seen only as coarse and weedy.

All have golden-yellow flowers in late
summer or autumn and all the ones worth
growing are of North American origin.
The seedheads are not particularly noteworthy,

but not to be rejected. Most of the winter
effect lies in the arrangement of supporting
stems rather than the tiny heads themselves,
or the fluffy seed which is rapidly blown away
when ripe.

Species and varieties Of the plume-shaped
heads that are commonest, those of *S. rugosa*
(Z3) are the most elegant, in both flower and
seed. *S. rigida* (Z4) has a stiff upright habit and
umbel-shaped heads.

Use Invaluable in large late-season borders and
wild gardens alongside asters, eupatoriums etc.

Sorghastrum Indian grass

POACEAE

Size and growth form Medium-sized to large
herbaceous perennial grass.

Persistence ❋ ❋

Sorghastrum nutans (Z4) is widely regarded as
one of the most beautiful of North American
prairie grasses, with large rich brown
flowerheads which mature to bronze
seedheads. Red-brown autumn colour can be
a feature, too. 'Sioux Blue' has glaucous
foliage. In northern and maritime climates,
a warm situation is vital.

following pages *Stipa calamagrostis* 'Lemperg' above *Stipa calamagrostis*

Use In prairie plantings. As a border plant it is a fine companion to large flowering perennials from midsummer on.

Sporobolus Dropseed

POACEAE

Size and growth form Medium-sized herbaceous perennial grass.

Persistence ✳✳

S. heterolepis, prairie dropseed (Z3), is another major prairie grass, but one more typical of the drier short-grass prairie zones. Tight tussocks of foliage and midsummer flowers, leading to ethereally airy seedheads. Foliage turns yellow-orange in autumn and bronze-cream in winter. Good on dry soils. *S. airoides* is similar, with similarly airy flower and seedheads. In northern and maritime climates, a warm situation is vital.

Use In prairie plantings but also highly effective in borders, where its very diffuse

visual texture is a valuable contrast to more defined forms. Particularly striking in front-of-border locations.

Stipa

POACEAE

Size and growth form Medium-sized to large herbaceous perennial grasses.

Persistence ✳/✳✳✳

Almost always natives of dry habitats across the temperate and desert zones of the globe, stipas have particularly delicate flower and seedheads, but vary considerably in size and visual effect. Like many other dryland plants, flowering is generally in early summer. The species mentioned do not seem to need sharper drainage than other grasses in common cultivation, and can be regarded as more reliable than pennisetums in cooler and maritime climes. They appear to start growth

at cooler temperatures than pennisetums and many prairie grasses, again making them more suitable for these climate zones.

Stipas are among the so-called 'bunch grasses' which dominated large areas of California and the American West, before being forced out of most of their habitat by more aggressive sod-forming European species and, in the case of the Central Valley – intensive irrigated agriculture. Their loss has been a largely unheralded ecological disaster, as upon their open growth depended many other species – flowering annuals in particular, as well as certain animals, such as bobwhite quail.

Species and varieties

S. gigantea (Z7) is the best known, with oat-like panicles on 2m stems. As the foliage only grows to around 50cm, in a tight clump, the plant has a 'transparent' quality. Backlighting against a dark background is almost essential

Stipa gigantea

for seeing it at its best, when sunlight turns each individual head into gold. Seedheads last from midsummer to early winter.

Persistence ✹ ✹

Use Most effective as an accent plant, surrounded by shorter neighbours.

S. pennata is 80cm tall with awns elongated into 30cm long plumes. *S. pulcherrima* is slightly larger (at 1m) and its 50cm long awns make it perhaps the most extraordinary ornamental grass of all: the awns ride every breath of air, and are consequently never at rest. Unfortunately both shed their seed within a couple of weeks of ripening, so they have a short season. Both are typical of east European and west Asian steppe habitats, where ground coverage is sparse; consequently the plants resent competition.

Persistence ✹

Use Very much accent or 'talking point' plants. Briefly spectacular if dotted around steppe or other low dry-habitat plantings.

S. tenuissima, Mexican feather grass (Z7), has profuse and dense plumes which somehow fit our romantic idea of what an ideal grass should be like. Very persistent, looking effective from

midsummer until late winter. Usually around 60cm high. In the opinion of some, it does not take post-winter clipping well, and is better 'combed' with a rake, to remove last season's spent heads. It is short-lived, often no more than three years, but self-sows well on lighter soils.

Persistence ✹ ✹ ✹

Use Highly effective as a single specimen, it is most useful as a dot plant among flowering perennials of a similar height to evoke wildflower meadow or as a mass planting.

S. brachytricha (Z5) – formerly classified under *Achnatherum* – is a quietly beautiful species with purple-flushed fawn-brown relatively tight flower panicles in later summer. The seedheads are pale brown and maintain the same posture – basically upright, but radiating out in an attractively relaxed way. *S. calamagrostis* (Z5) is very similar, but with a more floppy habit.

Persistence ✹ ✹

Use Very effective with similar-sized flowering herbaceous plants like species of *Monarda* and *Rudbeckia*.

Other *Stipa* species *S. capillata* (Z6, but almost certainly hardier than this) is a Eurasian steppe species, around 70cm tall, with stiff fine awns on its flower- and seedheads, which hang on for a few months. *S. ramosissima* (Z9) is an Australian species with flowers and seedheads in whorled panicles, giving the appearance of smoke. This is one of the largest of the genus – up to 2m high.

Stipa grasses are among the so-called 'bunch grasses' which dominated large areas of California and the American West, before being forced out of most of their habitat by more aggressive sod-forming European species and, in the case of the Central Valley – intensive irrigated agriculture. Their loss has been a largely unheralded ecological disaster, as upon their open growth depended many other species – flowering annuals in particular, as well as ceratin animals, such as bobwhite quail. Three very similar species, *S. cernua*, *S. lepida* and *S. pulchra* (all Z6), are all about 60cm tall with long feathery awns. All are decorative but have a relatively short season. They are possibly suitable for roofgreening projects, owing to their drought tolerance.

Succisa

DIPSACACEAE

Size and growth form Medium sized clump-forming herbaceous perennial.

Persistence ✹ ✹

S. pratensis (Z5) is a Eurasian species of poor damp soils. Blue flowers in tight heads in midsummer turn to small globular seedheads.

Use Most effective grown *en masse* in wildflower meadows.

Telekia

ASTERACEAE

Size and growth form Large clump-forming herbaceous perennials.

Persistence ✹ ✹

T. speciosa (Z6) is a robust plant of woodland-edge environments in central Europe, with golden-yellow daisies above bunches of large, coarse leaves in early summer. The seedheads are as solid-looking as the rest of the plants, their essential structure continuing to have a definite presence after the seed has blown away. The species tends to be short-lived but generally self-sows.

Use Wild gardens. Very effective in woodland-edge situations.

Thalictrum

RANUNCULACEAE

Size and growth form Species discussed are medium-sized to large or very large herbaceous perennials.

Persistence ✹ ✹

Thalictrums are plants of mountain and woodland-edge habitats across the Northern Hemisphere. They tend to flower in early summer, with loose panicles of small flowers in pink or mauve shades. Their foliage is divided into small leaflets and is very ornamental. Seed is held in small capsules aloft stiffly upright stems.

Species and varieties *T. aquilegiifolium* (Z5) is the best known, and most other species in cultivation are similar. *T. polygamum* is one of the tallest (at around 2m) and is particularly

Thalictrum rochebruneanum

Typha latifolia

Typha Reedmace

TYPHACEAE

Size and growth form Medium-sized to very large grass-like herbaceous perennials.

Persistence ✳✳✳

Many Northern Hemisphere temperate-zone ponds are fringed by a heavy growth of reedmace – often mistakenly called 'bulrushes'. Their neatly cylindrical rich brown heads are a notable feature of winter, gradually disintegrating into fluff-carrying seeds as winter progresses – as those who use them in winter flower arrangements often discover to their cost. All are extremely vigorous plants which can rapidly turn even a large garden pond into a swamp. Only the 80cm *T. minima* (Z4) is suitable for marginal planting in garden ponds; it has 5cm long flower-/seedheads.

Use As landscape elements in wetland habitats, where there is plenty of space. Can rapidly choke shallow water, but cannot establish in moving or deep water.

effective in small groups or scattered around the border.

Use Thalictrums are valued for their combination of early flower and height. As seedheads they are good companions for grasses, astrantias and other umbellifers.

Thermopsis

FABACEAE

Size and growth form Medium-sized clump-forming herbaceous perennials.

The yellow pea flowers of thermopsis are relatively early (June) compared to their many North American relatives, but they tend to be plants of different habitats – woodland edges and clearings. The foliage is divided into three leaflets and is attractive all season long, while the large brown seedheads are a good winter feature. However, they seem to be produced only when more than one genetically identical

individual is around for fertilization.

Persistence ✳✳

Use For larger borders or wild-garden plantings. The rapidly spreading roots of some species such as *T. montana* can be a disadvantage in the conventional border, but in prairie plantings this will not be a problem.

Tragopogon Goat's beard, salsify

ASTERACEAE

Size and growth form Medium-sized herbaceous perennials or annuals.

Persistence ✳

Tragopogons have a brief season of yellow or mauve daisy flowers in early summer which go on to produce spectacular but ephemeral giant 'dandelion clock' type seedheads. European or Mediterranean in origin.

Use Perhaps best regarded as a short-lived fun element.

Veratrum nigrum

Veratrum
LILIACEAE

Size and growth form Large herbaceous perennials.

Persistence 🌿🌿/🌿🌿🌿
Large pleated leaves are the main decorative characteristics of these mountain meadow plants. The tiny flowers are odd rather than beautiful and are densely crowded on to spikes; they are followed by swollen seed capsules, which stand the winter well. Z3–5.
Use Veratrums are very distinctive plants and add a touch of the noble and the unusual to borders.

Verbascum Mullein
SCROPHULARIACEAE

Size and growth form Species discussed are large to very large biennials or short-lived perennials.

Persistence 🌿🌿🌿
Mulleins are among the most valuable of all seedhead plants. Most produce a rosette of foliage in the first year, which in the case of those species with densely hairy leaves is quite decorative in its own right. Year two sees the production of a tall flower spike, the flowers producing hard little seed capsules. The spikes of seedheads are not only very decorative but remarkably strong, often standing for a second winter. All are from Europe and west Asia. Although biennial, they can usually be relied upon to self-sow, which in some cases can be rather too enthusiastically done.

Species and varieties Unless otherwise mentioned, flowers are yellow.
V. bombyciferum grows to 1.8m and has sparsely branched flower spikes; all surfaces are covered in a white woolly material.
V. olympicum is even taller (to 2m), with branched flower spikes and even more densely 'woolly'. *V. thapsus* is similar, but unbranched. *V. densiflorum* is somewhat shorter (to 1.6m) with branching spikes. *V. nigrum* grows to 90cm and is unbranched – this is the best species to 'let loose' by self-seeding in most garden borders. Most are Z5–6.
Use Highly effective in borders, gravel gardens and wild gardens; the dark colour and strong definition of the spikes against lighter and wispier winter remains is especially notable. Most dramatic of all is when self-seeding plants leave behind a forest of dark and gaunt spikes.

Verbena
VERBENACEAE

Size and growth form Those discussed are medium-sized to large short-lived perennials.
Persistence 🌿🌿/🌿🌿🌿
A few species are tall enough to make an impact in the winter, although this is due less to the very small seedheads than the overall effect of their stems.
Species and varieties North American *V. hastata* (Z3) is a sternly upright, rather ascetic-looking plant with small mauve flowers in dense spikes. Argentinian *V. bonariensis* (Z8) is an immensely long-flowering species which is best described as being 'nearly all stem',

Verbascum bombyciferum

Verbena hastata

Veronicastrum 'Temptation'

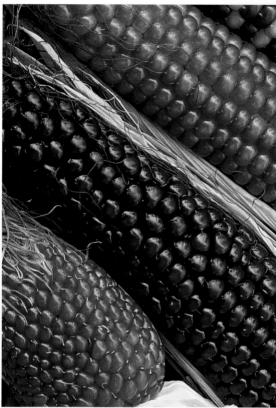

Zea mays

with tiny mauve flowers in rounded heads.
Use Both species described tend to sow
themselves around borders, but rarely become
a nuisance as they take up little room. Their
winter silhouettes can be particularly effective.

Vernonia Ironweed

ASTERACEAE

Size and growth form Species discussed are
very large clump-forming herbaceous
perennials.

Persistence ❋ ❋
Tall North American prairie plants with very
late violet flowers in umbels. Their dead
foliage is dark, an effective contrast to the
pale brown seedheads.
V. gigantea (Z4) is a spectacular 3m plus, the
seedheads best seen when backlit by winter
sun. Others are similar but shorter.
Use In borders and wild-garden plantings.
Effective with *Miscanthus* grasses.

Veronicastrum

SCROPHULARIACEAE

Size and growth form Large herbaceous
perennials.

Persistence ❋ ❋
It is the stiffly upright character of
veronicastrums that makes them such useful
plants in the border, over a long season. Tight
spikes of blue-mauve (or white or pink in the
case of cultivars) in early to midsummer are
followed by tiny seedheads – the main
decorative element being the stems. The
genus originates from North America and east
Asia. Z3.
Use Neat and predictable plants which always
creates a sense of order around them. Good
for combining with lower-growing and less
tidy herbaceous plants.

Zea Maize, corn

POACEAE

Size and growth form Large annual grass.
Persistence ❋ ❋ ❋
Ornamental varieties of *Zea mays* are
somewhat different to the other plants in this
book because they do not display their interest
on the plant, but only once picked, dehusked
and dried to be used in floral arrangements,
when the multicoloured kernels can be
appreciated. As with edible varieties, seed
should be sown, or young plants set out, only
once the soil is warm and any risk of frost is
passed.
Species and varieties A number of seed
strains have ornamental grains. 'Harlequin' has
red and white stripes on the foliage, and red
grains. 'Blue Jade' is a small-growing strain
with blue-black kernels, 'Indian Summer' has
mixed kernels: white, yellow, red and purple.

Index

Acknowledgments

As should be clear from the text, Piet Oudolf has done much to open my eyes to the beauty of plants in the winter, seedheads in particular, as has Henk Gerritsen with his very unorthodox and inspirational approach to garden making. The work of James van Sweden and Wolfgang Oehme in the USA has also been a great inspiration.

I would like to thank Anna Mumford for asking me to write the book, and Jo Whitworth for her photography. Thanks also to Penny David for her work on the text and Ruth Hope for designing it. And to my partner Jo Eliot, who is always behind me in my gardening, writing and research endeavours.